My Disney

STARS AND HEROES 2

Student's Book with eBook

Viv Lambert and Cheryl Pelteret

Scope and Sequence

Meet our Stars and Heroes!
page 4

Character introductions — I'm …, I like …, I can …
Let's have fun! song — Welcome back

	Vocabulary	Grammar and communication	Personal and Social Skills	Cross-curricular	Project and strategies
1 We are different page 10	**Adjectives** Appearance adjectives and nouns Abilities	Is she tall or short? She's tall. Does she have dark hair or red hair? She has dark hair. Does he have a beard? Yes, he does./No, he doesn't. **Ask and answer about what people can do** What can she do? She can horseback ride. She can't ride a scooter. Can she cook? Yes, she can./No, she can't.	**Social awareness:** Understanding the feelings of others *How do you feel?, It's OK.* **Story:** *Different is fun!*	**Art:** Drawing faces *chin, eyebrows, line, middle*	**Project:** 'My friend' poster **Self-management:** What I know vs what I can ask *I can ask … I know …*
2 At the ocean page 22	**Ocean words 1** Ocean words 2 Beach items	What's that? It's a sea lion. What are those? They're sea lions. **Ask and answer about possessions** Is this our home? Yes, it is./No, it isn't. Are these their shells? Yes, they are./No, they aren't.	**Self-management:** Knowing when to ask for help *alone, Can you help me, please?* **Story:** *The beach trip*	**Life Science:** The awesome octopus *change color, skin, suckers, weak*	**Project:** My ocean scene **Presentation skills:** Speaking loudly and clearly *Can you hear me?*
3 Around town page 34	**Things in the street** Places in town 1 Places in town 2	Is there a museum? Yes, there is./No, there isn't. Are there any trams? Yes, there are./No, there aren't. **Ask and answer about where things are** Where are they? They're in the bedroom. Where's the mall? It's across from the hotel.	**Self-management:** Persistence *bored, Don't give up!, I can't stop now., tired* **Story:** *The treasure hunt*	**Math:** 3D shapes in a city *cube, cuboid, cylinder, pyramid*	**Project:** My town poster **Self-management:** Sharing group tasks *I can draw …, task*
4 Let's eat page 46	**Food 1** Food 2 Meals and food	He likes soup. She doesn't like soup. Does she like tomatoes? Yes, she does./No, she doesn't. **Order and offer food** What would you like? I'd like some cake, please. Would you like some soup? Yes, please./No, thank you.	**Self-awareness:** Self-appreciation *I can … . I'm good at it!* **Story:** *Let's make some juice!*	**Science:** Food groups *carbohydrates, dairy, fats, fruit and vegetables, proteins*	**Project:** My food menu **Presentation skills:** Good role-play behavior *please, take turns, thank you*
5 The weather page 58	**Seasons** Weather Activities	What's the weather like? It's warm and sunny. It's very warm. **Ask and answer about seasonal activities** What do you do in winter? In winter, we play indoors.	**Relationship skills:** Listening to different ideas *listen to ideas, that's a great idea, work together* **Story:** *The kite*	**Life Science:** Ant life *bark, nest, team, underground*	**Project:** My activity tree **Self-management:** Following a plan *check, make, show*

Welcome — page 6

- Numbers 20–100
- Days of the week
- What time is it? It's 4 o'clock.
- It's Monday. On Mondays, I play soccer.
- **Social awareness:** Making new friends. Nice to meet you.

	Vocabulary	Grammar and communication	Personal and Social Skills	Cross-curricular	Project and strategies
6 My day page 70	Daily routines 1 Daily routines 2 Times of the day	We watch TV every day. They have dinner together. Do you exercise? Yes, we do./No, we don't. Do they exercise? Yes, they do./No, they don't. **Ask and answer about daily routines** When do you wake up? I wake up in the morning. I don't wake up at ten o'clock.	**Social awareness:** Helping at home help at home, be nice **Story:** Let's clean up!	**Science:** Night and day day, Earth, Moon, spin, Sun	**Project:** My activities clock **Presentation skills:** Speaking slowly and referring to the pictures point, speak fast, speak slowly
7 At work page 82	Jobs 1 Jobs 2 Work activities	What do you want to be? I want to be a baker. She wants to be a police officer. She doesn't want to be a farmer. **Ask and answer about people's jobs** What does she do? She's a farmer. She grows vegetables. She doesn't work at the police station.	**Self-awareness:** Self-efficacy dream big, work hard **Story:** The firefighter	**Technology:** Robots at work dangerous, heavy, lift, machines	**Project:** My dream job poster **Self-management:** Doing research for the project find out more, talk to someone, use a computer
8 After school page 94	Activities 1 Activities 2 Activities 3	They're reading a book. They aren't taking a nap. Are they listening to music? Yes, they are./No, they aren't. **Ask and answer about what people are doing** He's playing hide and seek. She isn't swinging. Is he sliding? Yes, he is./No, he isn't.	**Relationship skills:** Noticing how your behavior affects others feel bad, mean, sorry **Story:** The jigsaw puzzle	**Engineering:** How things fly air, engines, pressure, wings	**Project:** My free time poster **Presentation skills:** Practicing presentation practice, present
9 Party time page 106	Party items 1 Party activities Party items 2	What are you doing? I'm reading. What's Anna doing? She's listening. What are they doing? They're singing. **Say who things belong to** It's Anna's dress. They're Lucas's books.	**Responsible decision-making:** Party planning, sharing responsibilities be in charge, get ready, prepare **Story:** The party	**Art:** Rosemaling patterns curvy line, paintbrush, pattern, symmetry	**Project:** My cake design **Self-management:** Attitude and preparation I have what I need. I know what do to. I do my best.

Picture dictionary pages 118–127

Stickers and Cut-outs

Meet our Stars and Heroes!

1. 🎧 💬 Listen and point. Then point and say.

Sticker time

2. Collect your friend at the start of each unit!

Cinderella — W

- **Can:** dance
- **Friends:** birds and mice

Fergus — 1

- **Likes:** animals
- **Lives:** with his family

Dory — 2
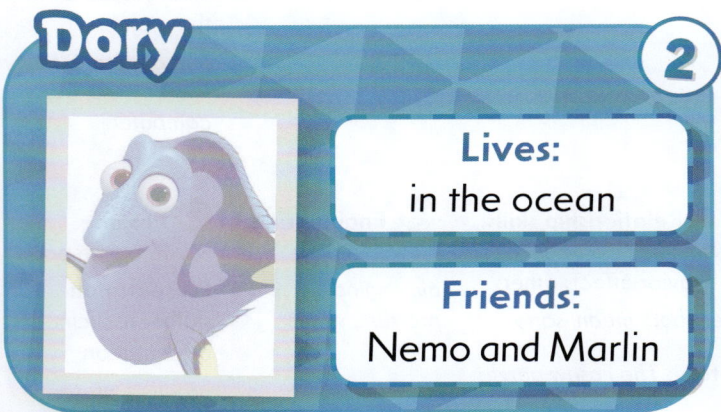
- **Lives:** in the ocean
- **Friends:** Nemo and Marlin

Hiro — 3

- **Likes:** robots
- **Family:** aunt Cass, brother Tadashi

Tiana — 4

- **Can:** cook
- **Friend:** Charlotte

Atta — 5

- **Family:** sister Dot
- **Friend:** Flik

Bob 6

- **Can:** drive a car
- **Lives:** with his family

Judy 7

- **Job:** police officer
- **Friend:** Nick

Lilo 8

- **Likes:** music
- **Friend:** Stitch

Olaf 9

- **Likes:** warm hugs
- **Friends:** Anna and Elsa

Sing-along

3 🎵 **Listen, sing, and act.**

Hello, hello, everyone!
Welcome back!
Let's have some fun.
Friends and heroes everywhere.
Welcome back!
Let's have some fun!

4 ✏️ 💬 **Be a hero. Write, draw, and say.**

Name: _____

I like _____
_____ .
I can _____
_____ .
My friends are
_____
_____ .

Welcome

LESSON 1 Time

1 🎧 💬 **Listen, point, and say. Then ask and answer.**

What time is it?

It's two o'clock.

2 ▶ **Watch the video. Check (✓). What time does Cinderella go home?**

① three o'clock ○   ② twelve o'clock ○   ③ eight o'clock ○

3 🎧 ✏️ **Listen and circle. Then draw.**

① It's **eight** / **three** o'clock.
② It's **ten** / **one** o'clock.
③ It's **five** / **nine** o'clock.

I can ask and answer about the time.

LESSON 2 Numbers

1 Watch again. Are Cinderella's sisters nice?

2 Listen, point, and say. Then ask a friend.

20 twenty **30** thirty **40** forty **50** fifty **60** sixty

70 seventy **80** eighty **90** ninety **100** a hundred

3 Listen and chant.

4 Listen and color. Then play.

84 72 45 100 31 66

Purple. Forty-five!

I can say numbers 20–100.

LESSON 3
Days of the week

1 🎧 💬 **Listen, point, and say. Then complete and ask a friend.**

Monday	Tuesday	Wednesday	Thursday	Friday	Saturday	Sunday

2 🎵 **Listen and chant.**

3 🎧 ✏️ **Listen and stick. Then write.**

Picture Dictionary page 118

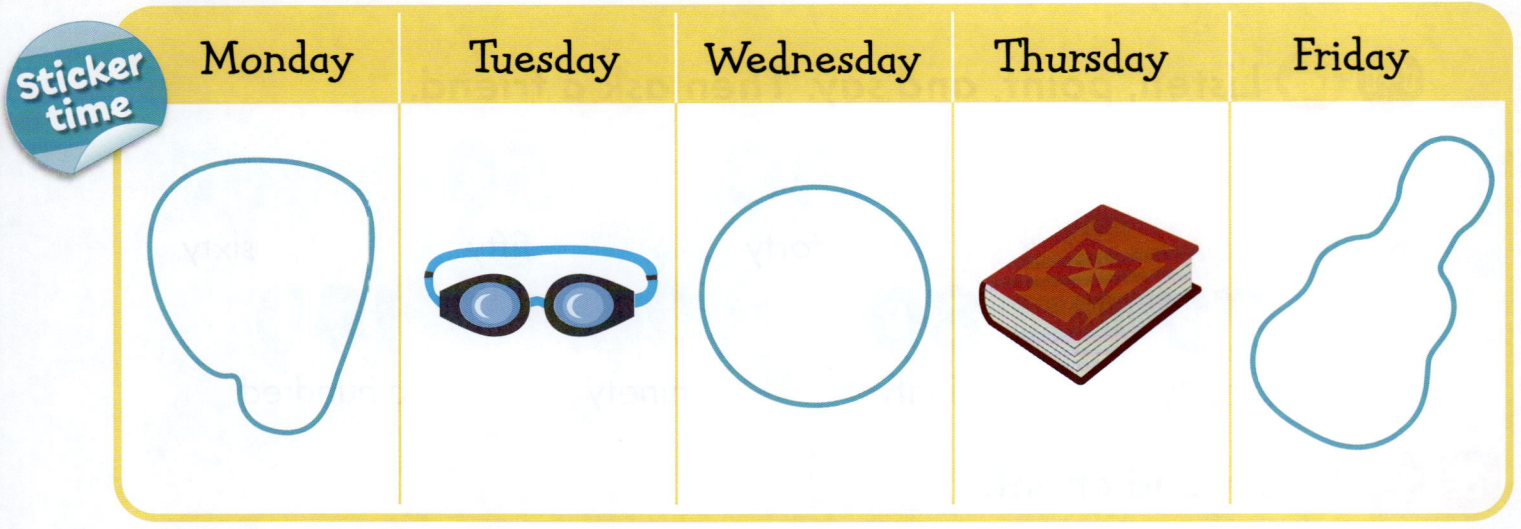

① On _____ , I jump rope.   ② On _____ , I swim.
③ On _____ , I play soccer. ④ On _____ , I play the guitar.

4 💬 **Ask and answer.**

What do you do on Saturdays?   On Saturdays, I play soccer.

I can name the days of the week.

Nice to meet you!

LESSON 4 — All about me

1. Listen and read. When does Amelia dance?

1. Hello. I'm Martina. I'm 26. I can play the guitar.
   Hi. My name's Pedro. I'm ten. This is my sister.
2. Hello! I'm Laura. I'm eight. I have 39 teddy bears!
   Wow!
3. What's your name?
   I'm Amelia. On Saturdays, I dance.
4. And I'm Niko! I swim before school on Mondays, Wednesdays, and Fridays! I get up at six o'clock.
   Wow! Nice to meet you all!

Make new friends!

2. Write the numbers in words.

8   6   10   26   39

1. Martina is _____ .
2. Laura is _____ .
3. Laura has _____ teddy bears.
4. Pedro is _____ .
5. Niko gets up at _____ o'clock.

3. Draw, write, and say.

I'm _____ . On Mondays, I _____ .

Nice to meet you!

I can share personal information.

LESSON 1 **Vocabulary**

3 🎧 💬 Listen, find, and say. Then ask a friend.

4 🎵 Listen, chant, and act.

fast

tall

short

I can describe people.

Collect your friend! page 4

LESSON 2
Vocabulary

1 🎧 1.3 💬 Listen, point, and say. Then play.

Eight. *Beard!*

 1 dark
 2 blond
 3 gray
 4 straight

 5 curly
 6 long
 7 glasses
 8 beard

2 🎧 1.4 💬 Listen and stick. Then play *Guess who?*

Sticker time

 1
 2
 3
 4

3 ✏️ 💬 Read and circle for you. Then draw and tell a friend.

1. I have **long** / **short** hair.
2. It's **blond** / **dark** / **red**.
3. It's **curly** / **straight**.
4. I **have** / **don't have** glasses.

Talk buddies

I have …

I can describe appearance.

LESSON 3
Grammar

1 🎧 1.5 **Listen and check (✓).**

🎧 1.6
Is she tall or short?
She's tall.
Does she have dark hair or red hair?
She has dark hair.
Does he have a beard?
Yes, he does./
No, he doesn't.

2 🎧 1.7 **Listen and say Yes or No.**

Grandpa

Mom

Billy

Betty

3 💬 **Cover the pictures in 2. Ask and answer.**

Does Grandpa have short hair or long hair?   He has short hair.

Does he have glasses?   No, he doesn't.

I can ask and answer about appearance.

LESSON 4
Story

Different is fun!

1 🎧 1.8 **Listen and read. What color hair does Daisy have?**

① Look! There's Amelia.

② Where's Daisy?

③ Are you OK, Daisy? Where's your picture?

It's here, but … only I have red hair.

④ But different is fun, Daisy! Look! Only Laura is tall.

Yes! And only Amelia has glasses.

⑤ Look! Daisy has red hair. And now I have red hair!

It's curly too!

⑥ Laura has long red hair!

Amelia has short red hair!

Smile!

Spot! Who has a beard?

2 ✏️ Read and circle.

1. Does Amelia have long or short red hair? She has **long** / **short** hair.
2. Is Laura tall or short? She's **tall** / **short**.
3. Who has glasses? **Daisy** / **Amelia** has glasses.
4. How many children have red hair at the end? **Three**. / **Seven**.

3 Read and check (✓).

1. How does Daisy feel at the beginning?

2. How does Daisy feel at the end?

4 💬 Act out the story.

Look! Only Laura is tall.

Yes! And only Amelia has glasses.

Talk buddies

I can read and understand a story.

LESSON 5
Vocabulary

1 🎧 1.9 💬 **Listen, point, and say. Then play.**

 1 cook
 2 horseback ride
 3 play basketball
 4 play the drums
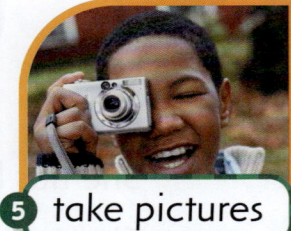 5 take pictures
 6 ride a scooter

Think and draw.
the drums
play
the guitar
soccer

Picture Dictionary page 119

2 🎧 1.10 💬 **Listen and say. Then play in pairs.**

 Take pictures!

Sing-along

3 🎵 1.11 **Listen, sing, and act.**

I can ride a scooter.
I can horseback ride.
But I can't play basketball
And I can't ride a bike.

*I'm not very tall.
I'm not very strong.
There are some things I can't do,
but I can sing this song!
I can sing this song, I can sing this song.
I can sing this song, I can sing this song.*

I can take pictures.
I can jump and run.
But I can't cook a pizza
And I can't play the drums.

Chorus

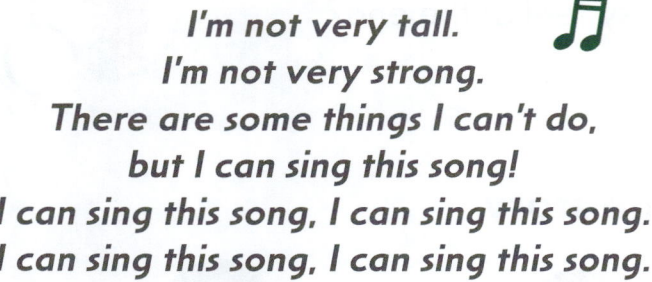

I can name free time activities.

Extra Lesson

Go online Phonics

LESSON 6
Grammar and Speaking

1 Watch the video. Check (✔). What can Merida do?

fly ◯   horseback ride ◯   climb ◯

> What can she do?
> She can horseback ride.
> She can't ride a scooter.
> Can she cook?
> Yes, she can./No, she can't.

2 Look, read, and write *Yes* or *No*. Then play in pairs.

Eva can ride a scooter.   Yes!

1. Eva can ride a scooter. _____
2. Eva can draw. _____
3. Eva can't dance. _____
4. Chris can't play basketball. _____
5. Chris can cook. _____
6. Chris can run fast. _____

Let's communicate!

3 Use the cut outs. Play the game.

Is it a girl or a boy?   It's a boy.

Can he cook?   No, he can't.

I can ask and answer about what people can do.

LESSON 7
Myself and others

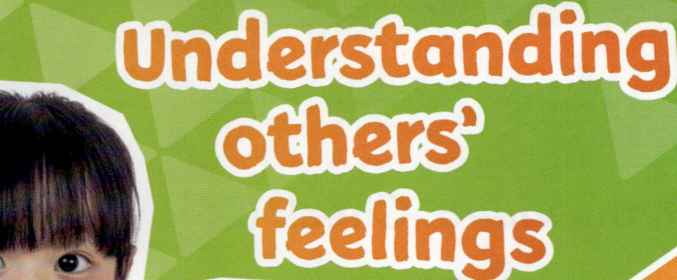

Understanding others' feelings

 **Listen and sing.** 🎵 1.13

🎵 I ask *How are you?*
Do you feel ok?
Are you happy or sad?
Do you want to play?

🎵 We're working hard,
We keep trying!
We are heroes,
We are heroes!

We're dreaming big,
We don't give up!
We are heroes,
We are heroes! 🎵

🎵 I talk to my friends,
Say *I'm here for you.*
Smile at them
and watch them smile, too.

🎵 **Chorus**

1 **Look and number. How do they feel?**

 a    b    c    d

① happy
② angry
③ excited
④ sad

2 🎧 1.14 **Listen and check (✓). Why do they feel this way?**

1  a    b   **2**  a   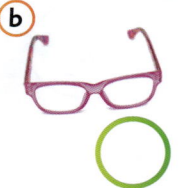 b   **3**  a   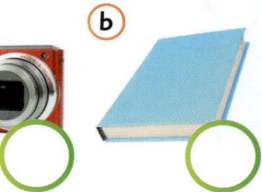 b

3 💡 **Look and circle. How does your friend feel today?**

 angry    sad    happy

 excited    worried

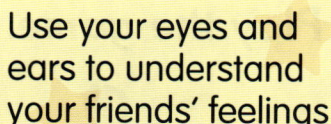 **Be a hero!**
Use your eyes and ears to understand your friends' feelings.

Social awareness I can say how someone feels.

Drawing faces

LESSON 8
My world

1 🎧 ✏️ **Let's explore!** Listen, read, and number.

Learn to draw faces! Use a pencil, a ruler, and an eraser.

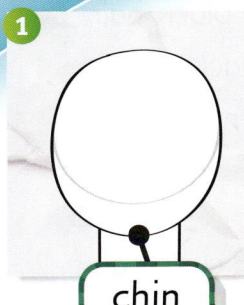 chin
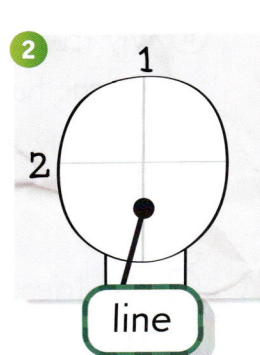 line
 eyebrows
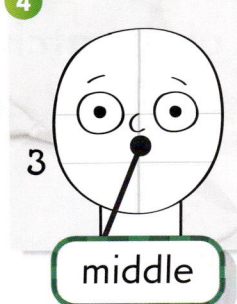 middle

a Draw the eyes on line 2. Now draw the **eyebrows**.

b Draw a circle. Then draw the **chin**. Use your eraser! ☐ 1

c Draw the nose in the **middle** of line 1, and then draw line 3 like this →.

d Draw the mouth on line 3. Now draw the hair and ears.

e Draw two lines: **line** 1 like this ↑ and line 2 like this →.

2 💡 **Think** Look and put a ✓ or ✗. Is it OK?

1. chin ○
2. ears ○
3. eyes ○
4. eyebrows ○
5. mouth ○
6. nose ○

3 ✏️ **Do** Look and say. Then draw one more. How can you show feelings?

Number 1 is sad.

I can read and understand about how to draw a face.

LESSON 9 Project

'My friend' poster

Let's review

1 ✏️ Read and match.

a. My friend has black hair. He can horseback ride and play soccer.

b. My friend has curly hair. He can't play soccer, but he can play basketball.

Get ready

2 🎧 1.16 Listen and check (✓) what Cleo knows about her friend.

- She has blond hair. ◯
- She can dance. ◯
- She has blue eyes. ◯
- She can ride a scooter. ◯

Workbook page 13

Create

3 🎨 Now make your poster. Write.

Reflect ☹ 🙂 😁

4 How did I do?
- I ask my friend. ◯
- I write about my friend. ◯
- I make my poster. ◯

I can make a poster and describe my friend.

I can do it!

LESSON 10 Review

1 **Read and number. Then ask and answer.**

Is Merida's mom short or tall?

1. She has long red hair.
2. He's tall. He's strong.
3. She's tall. She has straight hair.
4. He has short curly hair.

2 **Look and write *can* or *can't*. Then draw and say for you.**

1. Asta _____ ride a scooter.
2. She _____ play the drums.
3. She _____ play basketball.
4. She _____ take pictures.
5. She _____ cook.

3 **Think and check (✓). Then stick!**

I can ...
- describe people ☐
- read a story ☐
- sing a song ☐
- understand my friends' feelings ☐

Sticker time

I completed Unit 1!

Go online
Big Project

2 At the ocean

ocean

shark

Video story

1 Watch the video. Check (✓). Who does Dory want to find?

LESSON 1 **Vocabulary**

2 Watch again. Number in order. Who does Dory ask for help?

3 Listen, find, and say. Then ask a friend.

4 Listen, chant, and act.

octopus

boat

I can name ocean words.

Collect your friend!
page 4

23

LESSON 2
Vocabulary

1 🎧 2.3 💬 Listen, point, and say. Then play.

1. starfish

2. sea lion

3. shell

4. whale

5. dolphin

6. crab

7. jellyfish

8. beach

2 🎧 2.4 ✏️ Listen and stick. Then circle and say.

Sticker time

1. There's a **crab** / **jellyfish** on the beach.
2. There's a **sea lion** / **dolphin** under the boat.
3. There are three **whales** / **sharks**.
4. There are people **on the beach** / **in the boat**.

3 💬 Cover the picture in 2. Ask and answer.

Where's the sea lion?

It's on the rock.

Talk buddies

I can name ocean animals and things on the beach.

LESSON 3
Grammar

1 🎧 ✏️ Who's Gerald? Listen and check (✓). Then circle.

What's that?
It's a sea lion.
What are those?
They're sea lions.

They're / It's sea lions.

2 ✏️ Read and circle. Then write.

1.  What's **this / that**?
It's a _____ .

2.  What are **these / those**?
They're _____ .

3.  What are **these / those**?
_____

4.  What's **this / that**?
_____

3 💬 Point, ask, and answer.

What's that?

It's a whale.

I can ask and answer about what things are.

25

LESSON 4
Story

The beach trip

1 🎧 2.7 Listen and read. Which animals do the children help?

Spot! Can you find a dolphin?

7

Wow! Thanks, everyone.

The animals are happy now.

The end

2 Look, read, and write.

| bag   beach   crabs   ocean   starfish |

1. The _____ can run.
2. The _____ can't move.
3. The starfish is in the _____ .
4. Niko wants to play in the _____ .
5. The children clean the _____ .

3 Read and circle.

Pedro **can** / **can't** do it alone.

Pedro **can** / **can't** do it alone.

4 Act out the story.

But the beach is big.

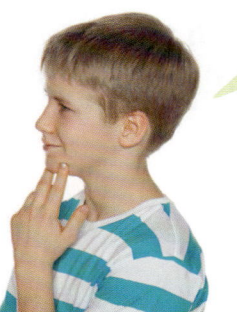

Wait! I have an idea.

Talk buddies

I can read and understand a story.

LESSON 5
Vocabulary

1 🎧 2.8 💬 Listen, point, and say. Then play.

1. bucket

2. towel

3. umbrella

4. sunhat

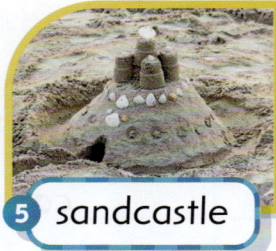
5. sandcastle

6. surfboard

In the ocean or on the beach?

on the beach
towel
surfboard
shark
in the ocean

Picture Dictionary page 120

2 🎧 2.9 💬 Look at 1. Listen and say Yes or No. Then play in pairs.

— The bucket is blue.
— No!

Sing-along

3 🎵 2.10 Listen, sing, and act.

Let's go to the beach today
Make a sandcastle, swim, and play!

Is this your umbrella?
Yes, it is. It's our umbrella.

Let's go to the beach today
Put a sunhat on, swim, and play!

Are these your buckets?
Yes, they are. They're our buckets.

Let's go to the beach today
Take a surfboard out, swim, and play!

Is this your towel?
Yes, it is. It's our towel.

Let's go to the beach today
Make a sandcastle, swim, and play!

I can name things on the beach.

Extra Lesson

Go online — Phonics

LESSON 6
Grammar and Speaking

1 Watch the video. Circle. What does Dory remember about her home?

rocks   shells   boats

Is this our home?
Yes, it is./No, it isn't.
Are these their shells?
Yes, they are./No, they aren't.

2 Listen and put a ✓ or ✗. Then circle and ask a friend.

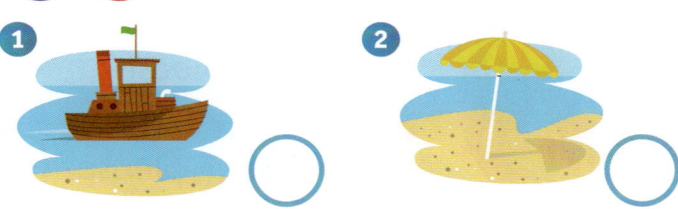

1. Jacob and Isa have a boat.
   Is that **our** / **their** boat?
2. We have an umbrella.
   Is that **our** / **their** umbrella?
3. Where are our buckets?
   Are those **our** / **their** buckets?
4. Where are their surfboards?
   Are those **our** / **their** surfboards?

Let's communicate!

3 Use the cut outs. Play the game.

Are these our buckets?

Yes, they are.

I can ask and answer about possessions.

LESSON 7
Myself and others

Asking for help

Listen and sing. 1.13

1 Check (✓) when Dory and Pedro ask for help.

2 2.13 Listen and number. Then read and check (✓).

a

b

c

1. Can you help me, please?

2. Can I do it, please?

3 Circle the good ways to ask for help.

Get angry.

Cry.

Ask a friend.

Say *please* and *thank you*.

Say what help I need.

Yell.
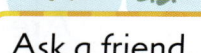

Be a hero!

Who can you ask for help? Make a "Helping Heroes" list.

Self-management I can ask for help.

30

The awesome octopus

LESSON 8
My world

1 🎧 **Let's explore!** Listen and read.
Why does an octopus change color?

suckers

The octopus is great at hiding. Its **skin** can **change color**. It can turn blue, gray, or green. Other animals can't see it, so they can't eat it.

The octopus has eight arms. Its arms aren't **weak**. They're very strong and they have **suckers** on them. The octopus can open shells with its arms.

The octopus doesn't have bones. Its body is soft, so it can hide in very small places.

2 💡 **Think** Read and circle.

1. The octopus can change its **skin** / **shell** color.
2. The octopus has **strong bones** / **a soft body**.
3. The octopus uses its arms to **open** / **close** shells.

3 ✏️ **Do** Look and write.

arms   ~~bones~~   ~~eyes~~   fingers
legs   skin   suckers

octopus   **me**

eyes   bones

I can read and understand about the octopus.

31

LESSON 9
Project

My ocean scene

Let's review

1 🎧 2.15 **Read and match. Then listen and circle.**

a. There are crabs on the beach.

b. There's a jellyfish in the ocean.

Get ready

2 🎧 2.16 **Listen and check (✔). What does Lena do this time?**

She takes a deep breath. ◯   She sits down. ◯

She speaks loudly. ◯   She speaks clearly. ◯

Workbook page 25

Create

3 🎨 💬 Now make your ocean scene. Then tell the class.

Reflect ☹ 🙂 😀

4 How did I do?

I speak loudly. ◯

I speak clearly. ◯

I present my project. ◯

I can make and present an ocean scene.

**LESSON 10
Review**

I can do it!

1 🖊️ 💬 **Look, read, and number. Then ask and answer.**

1. octopus
2. sea lion
3. bucket
4. shell
5. boat
6. umbrella
7. shark
8. sandcastle

2 🖊️ **Read and circle.**

1. What's **that** / **those**? It's a house.
2. Do Dory's parents live here?
   Is it **our** / **their** house?
3. What are **that** / **those**? They're turtles.
4. Look at the turtles! Dory and Nemo are **our** / **their** friends.

3 💡 **Think and check (✔). Then stick!**

I can ...

- 💬 name ocean animals and things on the beach ☐
- 📖 read a story ☐
- 🎵 sing a song ☐
- 🙋 ask for help ☐

Sticker time

✅ **I completed Unit 2!**

Go online
Big Project

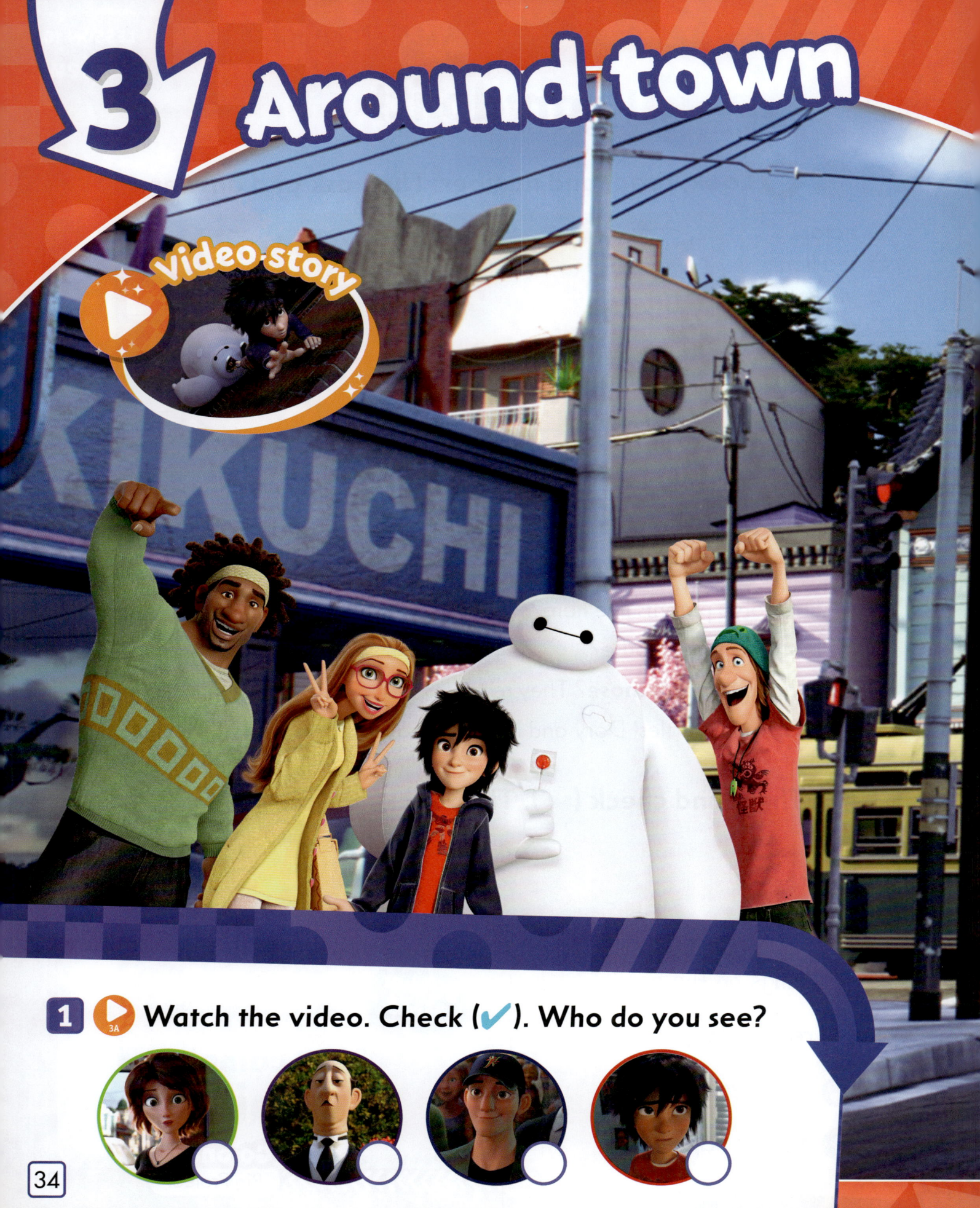

3 Around town

1 Watch the video. Check (✓). Who do you see?

LESSON 1 **Vocabulary**

2 Watch again. Check (✓). What do Tadashi and Hiro say when they're tired?

- I can do this. ○
- I can stop now. ○
- I can't do this. ○
- I can't stop now. ○

3 Listen, point, and say. Then ask a friend.

1. street
2. truck
3. tram
4. bus

4 Listen, chant, and act.

I can name things on the street.

Collect your friend! page 4

LESSON 2
Vocabulary

1 🎧 3.3 💬 Listen, point, and say. Then play.

1. grocery store

2. train station

3. museum

4. movie theater

5. bookstore

6. hospital

7. restaurant

8. fire station

2 🎧 3.4 ✏️ Listen and number.

3 ✏️ Look at 2. Find and circle five differences.

4 💬 Play the game.   There's a train station.   Blue Street.

I can name places in town.

LESSON 3
Grammar

1 🎧 3.5 ✏️ **Listen and circle.**

Are there any red buses?

Yes, there are. / No, there aren't.

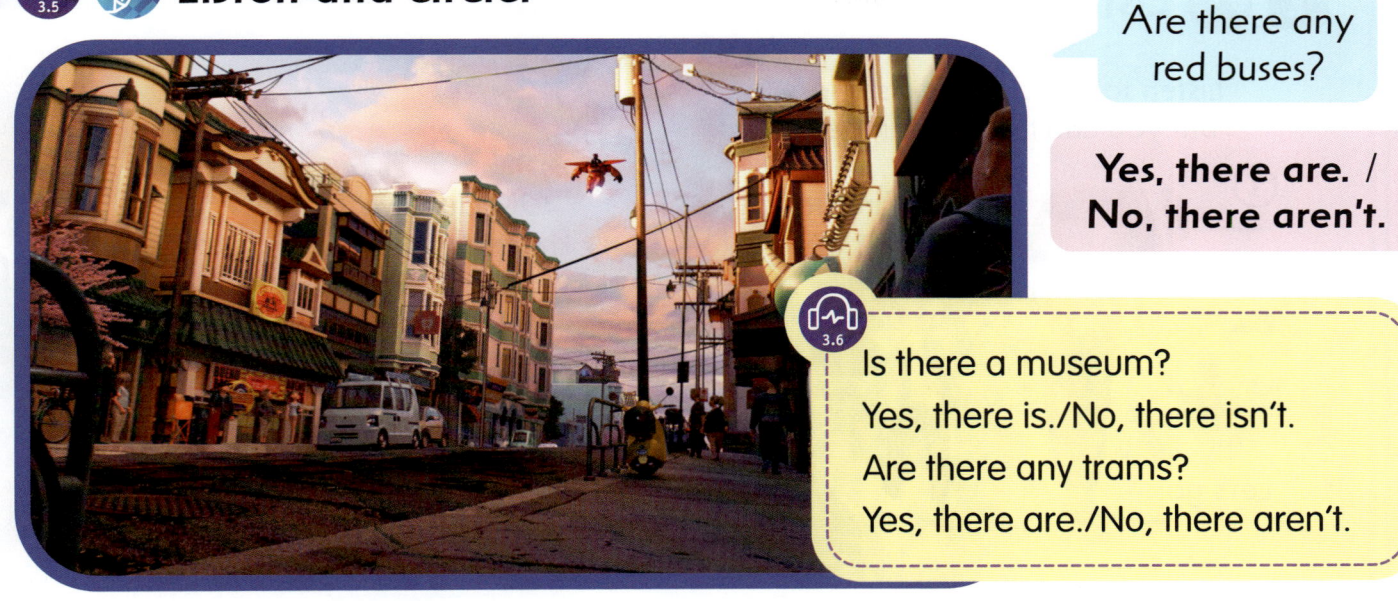

🎧 3.6
Is there a museum?
Yes, there is./No, there isn't.
Are there any trams?
Yes, there are./No, there aren't.

2 🎧 3.7 💬 **Listen and stick. Then ask and answer.**

Sticker time

1. Newtown
2. Freetown
3. Townsville

3 💬 **Ask and answer questions about your town.**

Are there any restaurants?

Yes, there are.

Talk buddies

I can ask and answer about places in town.

37

LESSON 4
Story

The treasure hunt

1 🎧 3.8 Listen and read. Where are the dinosaurs?

1 Listen to this clue. It's a station, but you can't see a train here.
— I know! Fire station!
— Let's go!

2 OK, clue two. There's food here.
— Grocery store?
— There isn't a grocery store here, but there's a restaurant! Come on!

3 Oh! Niko and Laura are already here. I'm tired.
— Come on, Pedro. We can do it! What's the clue?

4 You can see dinosaurs here.
— Ah! There are dinosaurs at the museum. Let's go!

5 Are there any clues here?
— No, there aren't.
— I'm bored now.
— Don't give up, Amelia. Think!

6 I know! The movie theater!
— Quick! Run!

Spot! Can you find two trucks?

⑦ Good job, Amelia. Good job, Pedro. These are for you!

Oh, wow! Thanks, Dad!

The end

2 Put a ✓ or ✗. Where do Pedro and Amelia go?

1. MOVIES
2. GROCERY STORE
3. MUSEUM
4. Restaurant
5. FIRE STATION

3 ✏️ Read and number. What do they say?

a. I'm tired.
b. I'm bored.
c. We can do it.
d. Don't give up!

4 💬 Act out the story.

I'm bored now.

Don't give up!

Talk buddies

I can read and understand a story.

LESSON 5
Vocabulary

1 🎧 3.9 💬 **Listen, point, and say. Then play.**

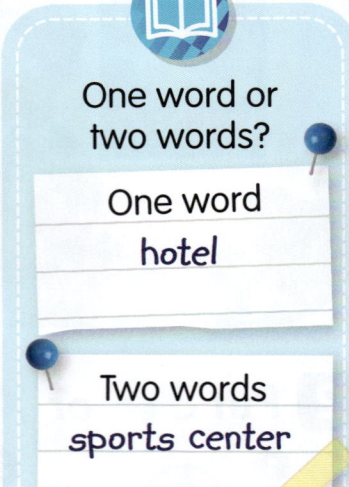

1. sports center
2. apartment building
3. hotel
4. mall
5. factory
6. police station

One word or two words?

One word
hotel

Two words
sports center

Picture Dictionary page 121

2 🎧 3.10 💬 **Listen and say. Then play in pairs.**

Hotel!

Sing-along

3 🎵 3.11 **Listen, sing, and act.**

Look at us! We're on the school bus.
Wave at us! We're on the yellow bus!

That's our apartment building. It's very tall.
There's the sports center, there's the mall.

Chorus

There's the police station, the hotel, too.
That's the factory. It's big and new.

Chorus

There's the fire station, see the red trucks.
Oh! Here's our school! Please stop the bus!

Chorus

I can name places in town.

Extra Lesson

Go online — Phonics

LESSON 6
Grammar and Speaking

1 🎬 ✏️ Watch the video. Check (✓). Where's Hiro?

kitchen ○

bedroom ○

living room ○

🎧 3.12
Where is he?
He's between the bed and the chair.
Where are they?
They're in the bedroom.
Where's the mall?
It's across from the hotel.

2 🎧 ✏️ Listen and number. Then ask and answer.

① movie theater ② sports center ③ bookstore

Where's the hospital?

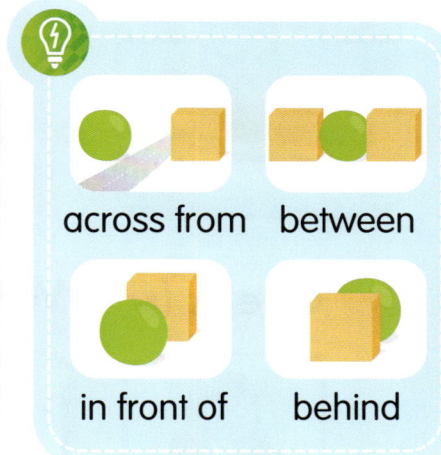

💡
across from | between
in front of | behind

Let's communicate!

3 💬 Use the cut outs. Play the game.

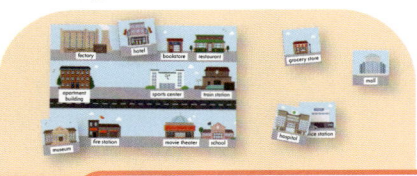

✂️ Cut outs

Where's the school?

It's across from the train station.

I can ask and answer about where things are.

41

LESSON 7
Myself and others

Listen and sing. 1.13

Keep trying!

1 Look and say. What is hard for them?

2 🎧 3.14 Listen, check (✓), and say.

1. I can't do it. I'm tired.
   I can do it. I can't stop now.

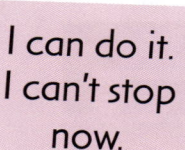

2. We can't find it. Let's go home.
   Don't give up. Let's look at the map.

3 Check (✓). When do you feel tired or bored?

4 💡 ✏️ Circle. What can you say to keep trying?

- I'm bored.
- I can do it.
- I can't do it.
- Don't give up.

Be a hero!
Give yourself points for every hard thing you do this week!

Self-management I can keep trying.

3D shapes in a city

Math — LESSON 8 — My world

1 🎧 3.15 ✏️ **Let's explore!** Listen, read, and number.

a) This house is a **cube**. All the sides are the same. They're square. ☐

b) There are a lot of shapes in towns and cities. This is a **pyramid**. Its sides are four triangles. ☐

c) Some apartment buildings are **cuboids**. Their sides are rectangles. Some are tall, and some are short. This apartment building is a big cuboid. ☐

d) **Cylinders** are tall circles. This hotel is in a very tall cylinder. The bedrooms aren't square! ☐

2 💡 ✏️ **Think** Read and write.

> cube   cuboid   cylinder   pyramid

1. You can find triangle shapes in a _____ .
2. A _____ is a tall circle.
3. A _____ has rectangle sides.
4. Six squares make a _____ . All the sides are the same.

3 ✏️ **Do** Count and write.

cylinders ☐   cuboids ☐
cubes ☐   pyramids ☐

I can read and understand about 3D shapes.

43

LESSON 9
Project

My town poster

Self-management

Let's review

1 🖊 **Look and write.**

1. The hospital is between the hotel and the _____ .
2. The museum is _____ the hotel.
3. The mall is _____ the hospital.
4. The school is _____ the sports center.

Get ready

2 🎧 3.16 🖊 **Listen and match.**

1. Eve   a) sports center and hotel
2. Lin   b) hospital and train station
3. Cam   c) museum and school

Workbook page 37

Create

3 🎨 Now make your poster. Write.

Reflect ☹ 🙂 😃

4 How did I do?

I share group tasks.   ◯

I do my task.   ◯

I create my poster.   ◯

I can make a poster and write about my town.

LESSON 10
Review

I can do it!

1 Look and write. Then listen and number.

factory   police station   restaurant   tram

a. _____
b. _____
c. _____
d. _____

2 Look and draw. Then ask your friend.

Is there a hotel?

3 Think and check (✓). Then stick!

I can ...
- name places in town
- read a story
- sing a song
- keep trying

Sticker time

✓ I completed Unit 3!

Go online
Big Project

45

4 Let's eat

peas

potatoes

cake

video story

1 ▶ **Watch the video. Check (✔). What do you see?**

46

LESSON 1 Vocabulary

2 Watch again. Circle. What can Tiana do?

3 Listen, find, and say. Then ask a friend.

4 Listen, chant, and act.

soup

I can name food.

Collect your friend!
page 4

47

LESSON 2
Vocabulary

1 🎧 4.3 💬 Listen, point, and say. Then play.

1. lemons
2. kiwis
3. nuts
4. chocolate
5. chicken
6. mangoes
7. pineapples
8. yogurt

2 🎧 4.4 💬 Listen and say. Then play.

They're small and yellow.

Lemons!

3 ✏️ Look and write.

1. _____
2. _____
3. _____
4. _____

4 💬 Play the game.

I have lemons.

I have lemons and mangoes.

I have lemons, mangoes, and chicken.

Talk buddies

I can name food.

48

LESSON 3
Grammar

1 Listen and circle.

He likes soup.
He loves yogurt.
She doesn't like soup.
Does she like tomatoes?
Yes, she does./
No, she doesn't.

Tiana **likes** / **doesn't like** soup.

2 Listen and stick. Then write.

Sticker time

a He _____ kiwis.
b He _____ lemons.

a She _____ peas.
b She _____ chocolate.

3 Look at 2. Play the game.

He likes lemons.   No, he doesn't!

Talk buddies

I can say what people like and don't like.

49

**LESSON 4
Story**

Let's make some juice!

1 🎧 4.8 **Listen and read. What can Niko do?**

① Wow, Will! Your cookies are great!

Thanks. I can't cook, but I *can* make cookies!

Yum!

Pedro likes chocolate!

② Pedro, can you draw kiwis and lemons?

Yes! I can draw juice and cookies, too.

③ Hey, Niko! Come and help us.

Sorry! I can't help you. I can't draw and I can't cook!

④ Does Oscar like pineapples?

Yes, he does. He likes kiwis, mangoes, and bananas, too. He doesn't like lemons.

⑤ Oh, no! We need a new blender.

I can help. I can ride a bike fast!

Spot! How many lemons can you find?

6 Ten minutes later …

Good job, Niko! Thank you!

You're welcome!

The end

2 ✏️ **Read and write Yes or No.**
1. Will has lemon cookies. _____
2. Pedro likes chocolate. _____
3. Laura makes juice. _____
4. Oscar likes lemons. _____

3 ✏️ **Read and write. What can they do?**

1. I can make _____ .
2. I can _____ .
3. I can _____ fast.
4. We can make _____ .

4 💬 **Act out the story.**

Wow, Will! Your cookies are great!

Thanks.

Talk buddies

I can read and understand a story.

LESSON 5
Vocabulary

1 🎧 4.9 💬 Listen, point, and say. Then play.

1. breakfast
2. lunch
3. dinner
4. cereal
5. burger
6. fries

Draw times for you.

breakfast

Picture Dictionary page 122

2 🎧 4.10 💬 Listen and check (✔) in 1. Then ask and answer.

What time do you have breakfast?

I have breakfast at eight o'clock.

Sing-along

3 🎵 4.11 Listen, sing, and act.

I'm hungry. What's for breakfast?
I'm hungry. What's for lunch?
I'm hungry. What's for dinner?
I'm hungry. Munch, munch, munch!

Yogurt and cereal. That's breakfast.
Bread and jam. That's lunch!
Burger and fries. That's dinner.
Now some chocolate. Munch, munch, munch!

I'm hungry. What's for breakfast?
I'm hungry. What's for lunch?
I'm hungry. What's for dinner?
I'm hungry. Munch, munch, munch!

I can name food and meals.

Extra Lesson

Go online
Phonics

LESSON 6
Grammar and Speaking

1 Watch the video. Circle. What would Mr. La Bouff like?

pizza   cake   burger and fries

> 4.12
> What would you like?
> I'd like some cake, please.
> Would you like some soup?
> Yes, please./No, thank you.

2 Listen and match. Then play.

1. Aisha
2. Juan
3. Matt

> Would you like some chicken?
> Yes, please.
> You're Juan!

a. b. c. d.

Let's communicate!

3 Use the cut outs. Play the game.

Cut outs

> Would you like some yogurt for breakfast?
> No, thank you.

I can ask and answer about what food I would like.

53

LESSON 7
Myself and others

Recognizing strengths

Listen and sing. 🎵 1.13

1 ✏️ Look and match. What can they do?

1 2 3 4

a b c d

2 🎧✏️ Listen and check (✓). Then write for George. 4.14

1 2 3

I can _____
_____ .
I'm good at it.

3 💡✏️ Choose and write or think of your own ideas.

I'm _____
_____ .
I can _____
_____ .

a good friend
kind   funny
draw   sing
cook

Be a hero!

Look at your friend's mirror. Say something nice about your friend.

You can make great cookies.

Self-awareness I can say what I'm good at.

54

Food groups

LESSON 8
My world
Science

1 🎧 ✏️ **Let's explore!** Listen, read, and match.

a b c d e

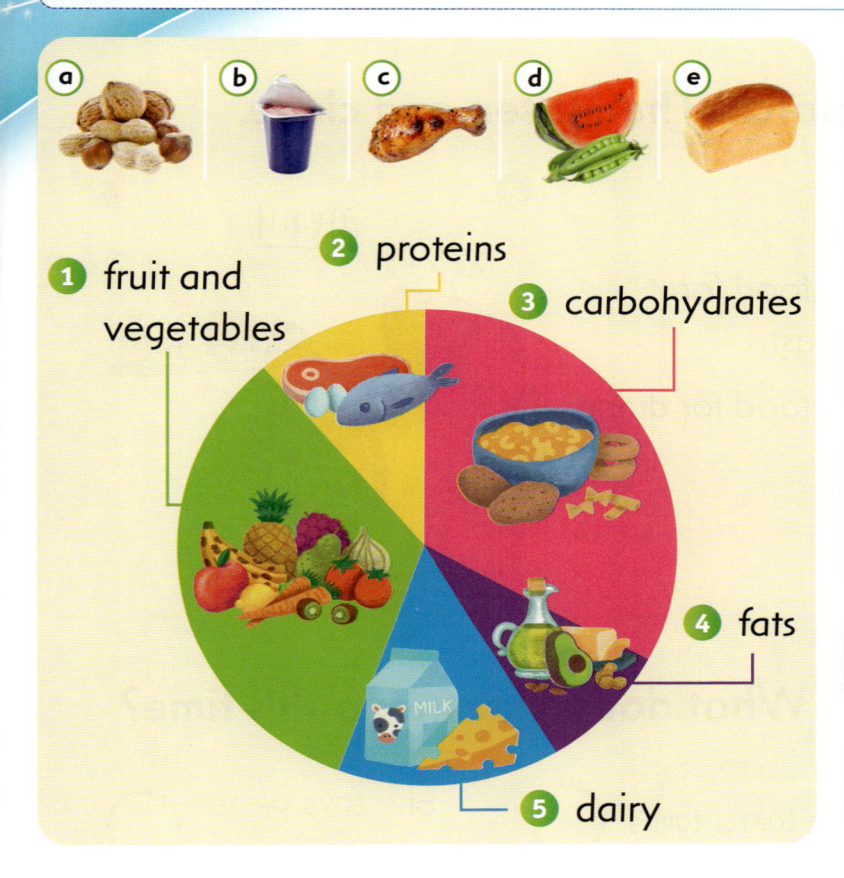

1. fruit and vegetables
2. proteins
3. carbohydrates
4. fats
5. dairy

Fruit and vegetables: Eat five different fruit and vegetables every day. You can eat tomatoes, pineapples, and peas. They have a lot of good things in them.

Proteins: Eat meat, fish, and eggs for strong muscles.

Carbohydrates: Do you play sports? Eat bread, potatoes, and noodles to have energy.

Fats: Some fats are good for you. Nuts have good fats.

Dairy: Milk, yogurt, and cheese give you strong bones.

2 💡 ✏️ **Think** Read and circle. Then write one more.

1. Fats: **fruit** / **nuts**
2. Carbohydrates: **milk** / **rice** and _____
3. Dairy: **eggs** / **cheese** and _____
4. Fruit and vegetables: **onions** / **cake** and _____
5. Proteins: **chicken** / **potatoes** and _____

3 ✏️ 💬 **Do** Draw your favorite dinner. Say the food groups.

I can read and understand about food groups.

LESSON 9 Project

My food menu

Presentation

Let's review

1 🎧 4.16 **Look, read, and match. Then listen and circle.**

1.
a. This is food for breakfast.
b. This is food for dinner.

2.

Get ready

2 🎧 4.17 **Listen and check (✓). What does Marina do this time?**

- She listens to her friend. ◯
- She takes turns. ◯
- She says *please* and *thank you*. ◯

Workbook page 49

Create

3 Now make your menu. Then act out with a friend.

What would you like?

I'd like a pizza, please.

Reflect ☹ 🙂 😁

4 How did I do?

- I make my project. ◯
- I listen to my friend. ◯
- I take turns. ◯
- I say *please* and *thank you*. ◯

I can make a menu and act out a scene.

LESSON 10
Review

I can do it!

1 🎧 💬 **Listen and put a ✓ or ✗. Then say.**

1. (pineapples)
2. (lemons)
3. (yogurt)
4. (chicken)
5. (burger)
6. (peas)
7. (potatoes)
8. (fries)
9. (chocolate)

> She likes pineapples.

> She doesn't like lemons.

2 ✏️ 🎧 **Read and write. Then listen and check.**

like   please   thank you   would

1. Good afternoon. What _____ you like?
2. I'd like some soup, _____ .
3. Would you _____ some bread?
4. No, _____ .

3 💡 **Think and check (✓). Then stick!**

I can ...
- 💬 name food items ☐
- 📖 read a story ☐
- 🎵 sing a song ☐
- 🌟 name my strengths ☐

Sticker time

Test your progress with English Benchmark Young Learners

✓ I completed Unit 4!

Go online
Big Project

5 The weather

Video-story

summer

spring

fall

LESSON 1 Vocabulary

1 ▶ 5A Watch the video. Check (✓) the animals you see.

2 ▶ 5A Watch again. Circle. Who likes Flik's ideas?

Atta   Dot

3 🎧 5.1 💬 Listen, find, and say. Then ask a friend.

4 🎵 5.2 Listen, chant, and act.

winter

I can name the seasons.

Collect your friend! page 4

59

LESSON 2
Vocabulary

1 🎧 💬 **Listen, point, and say. Then play.**

1. sunny
2. rainy
3. windy
4. snowy
5. cloudy
6. stormy
7. warm
8. cool

2 🎧 **Listen and stick.**

Sticker time

Monday	Tuesday	Wednesday	Thursday	Friday	Saturday	Sunday
☔		🍂		☁️		☀️🌡️

3 ✏️ **Look at 2 and write.**

1. On Monday, it's _____ .
2. On Wednesday, it's _____ .
3. On Friday, it's _____ .
4. On Sunday, it's _____ .

4 💬 **Play the game.**

It's cloudy.

Friday!

Talk buddies

I can describe the weather.

LESSON 3
Grammar

1 🎧 ✏️ **Listen and circle.**

It's cool.   It's warm.
It's cold.

🎧 What's the weather like?
It's warm and sunny.
It's very warm.

2 ✏️ 🎧 **Look and write. Then listen and number.**

fall   spring   summer   winter

a   b   c   d

It's _____ .   It's _____ .   It's _____ .   It's _____ .

3 💬 **Play Guess the season!**

What's the weather like?   It's cool and windy.

It's fall.

Talk buddies

I can ask and answer about the weather.

LESSON 4
Story

The kite

1 🎧 5.8 Listen and read. What's the weather like?

① It's very windy!
Oh, no! Look at the kite!

② I can climb the tree!
Thanks, Niko, but the tree is too tall.
I have another idea.

③ Uff! It's heavy. I can't do it. My idea doesn't work.
I have an idea, too!

④ Come on! Let's work together. One, two, three … Pull!

⑤ Ouch!
But we have our kite! Thanks, Pedro.

Spot! What can birds eat in the park?

⑥ Oh, no! Look at the weather. It's rainy now.

Wait! Now *I* have an idea.

⑦ It's an umbrella now.

That's a great idea, Laura.

We *all* have great ideas!

The end

2 ✏️ **Read and number the ideas in order.**

a. make an umbrella
b. climb the tree
c. move the table
d. pull the kite

3 **Check (✓). When do they work together?**

4 💬 **Act out the story.**

It's very windy!

Oh, no! Look at the kite!

Talk buddies

I can read and understand a story.

LESSON 5
Vocabulary

1 🎧 5.9 💬 **Listen, point, and say. Then play.**

1. fly a kite
2. plant seeds 
3. go to the park 
4. make snowballs 
5. go sledding 
6. play indoors 

📖 What can you do? It's fall.

fly a kite

It's winter.

make snowballs

Picture Dictionary page 123

2 🎧 5.10 💬 **Listen and say. Then play in pairs.**

It's rainy and cold.

Play indoors.

Sing-along

3 🎵 5.11 **Listen, sing, and act.**

It's sunny today. Let's go to the park.
We can ride our bikes and fly our kites!

We can have fun, in the rain or sun!
We can have fun, in the rain or sun!

It's warm today. Let's play in the yard.
We can plant some seeds: carrots and peas!

Chorus

It's rainy today. Let's play indoors.
We can read a book and eat chicken soup!

Chorus

It's snowy today. We can't go to the mall.
Let's go sledding and make snowballs!

Chorus

I can name seasonal activities. Extra Lesson Go online Phonics

LESSON 6
Grammar and Speaking

1 Watch the video. Write. What season is it?

In _____ , the ants play outside.

What do you do in winter?
In winter, we play indoors.

2 Listen and number. Then ask and answer.

What do you do in winter?   In winter, we make snowballs.

a   b    c 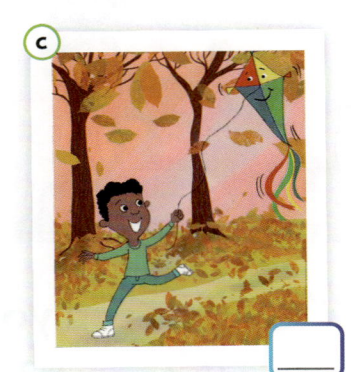   d

Let's communicate!

What do you do in fall?

In fall, we play indoors.

3 Use the cut outs. Play the game.

cut outs

I can ask and answer about seasonal activities.

LESSON 7
Myself and others

Sharing ideas

Listen and sing. 1.13

1 Look and check (✓). Which ideas work?

2 🎧 💬 Listen and say. Which idea do the children like?
5.14

3 💡 Check (✓). What can you do when you work with friends?

Say *I don't like your idea.*

Listen to all ideas.

Work together.

Say *Your idea doesn't work.*

Get angry.

Be a hero!

Who do you work together with? Tell a friend.

66   **Relationship skills** I can work together with others.

Ant life

LESSON 8
Life Science
My world

1 🎧 ✏️ **Let's explore!** Listen, read, and number.
5.15

a. Their nests are in the **bark** of trees, **underground**, or under rocks. It's warm in their nests.

b. In winter, it's cold. The ants sleep in their nests.

c. In summer and fall, ants find food. They eat a lot and their bodies are strong. They work in **teams**. They find leaves and grass to make **nests**.

underground
team
bark
nest

2 💡 ✏️ **Think** Match. What do ants do in summer and in winter?

1. eat a lot
2. make a nest
3. find food
4. sleep

a. summer
b. winter 

3 ✏️ **Do** Check (✔). Where can't ants build a nest?

1. 2. 3. 4. 5.

I can read and understand about the life of an ant.

67

LESSON 9
Project

My activity tree

self-management

Let's review

1 ✏️ **Look and write.**

1. In _____, I play soccer.
2. In summer, I _____.
3. In fall, I _____.
4. In _____, I make snowballs.

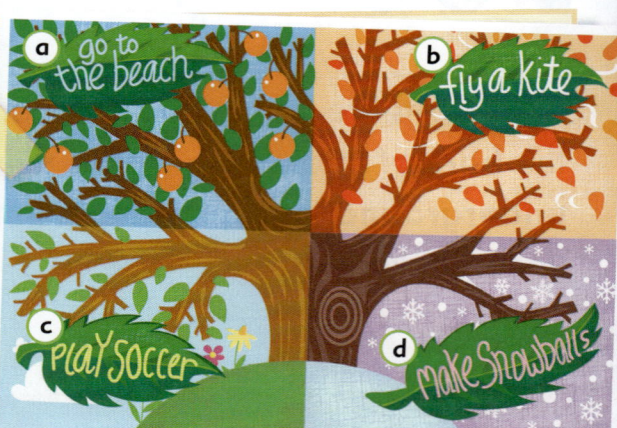

a. go to the beach
b. fly a kite
c. play soccer
d. make snowballs

Get ready

2 ✏️ **Read and number in order. Then write.**

Get my things
paper, _____
_____
_____

Check
Read and check my spelling.

Show
Show my project to the teacher.

Make
1 Draw my tree.
2 Make the leaves.
3 Write activities on the leaves.
4 Put the leaves on the tree.

Workbook page 61

Create

3 🎨 **Now make your tree. Write.**

Reflect ☹️ 🙂 😄

4 **How did I do?**

I plan my project. ⚪
I make my project. ⚪
I check my project. ⚪
I show my project. ⚪

I can make and describe an activity tree.

**LESSON 10
Review**

I can do it!

1 ✏️ 🎧 5.16 **Look and write. Then listen and number.**

cloudy   rainy   snowy   stormy   windy

a b c d e

2 ✏️ 💬 **Look and write. Then say in pairs.**

fall   go (x2)   plant   play   spring   summer   winter

1 In _____ , we _____ seeds.
2 In _____ , we _____ to the park.
3 In _____ , we _____ indoors.
4 In _____ , we _____ sledding.

Winter!   Go sledding!

3 💡 **Think and check (✓). Then stick!**

I can ...
- 💬 describe the weather and things I do
- 📖 read a story
- 🎵 sing a song
- 🧍 work together

Sticker time

✓ I completed Unit 5!

Go online
Big Project

6 My day

video story

go to work

do homework

watch TV

LESSON 1 **Vocabulary**

1 ▶ Watch the video. Check (✓). Where does Mom go?

to a restaurant ○   to work ○   to school ○

2 ▶ ✎ Watch again. Match. How do they help?

a
b
c

1 cook, clean, help the children
2 go to school
3 go to work

3 🎧 💬 Listen, find, and say. Then ask a friend.

4 🎵 Listen, chant, and act.

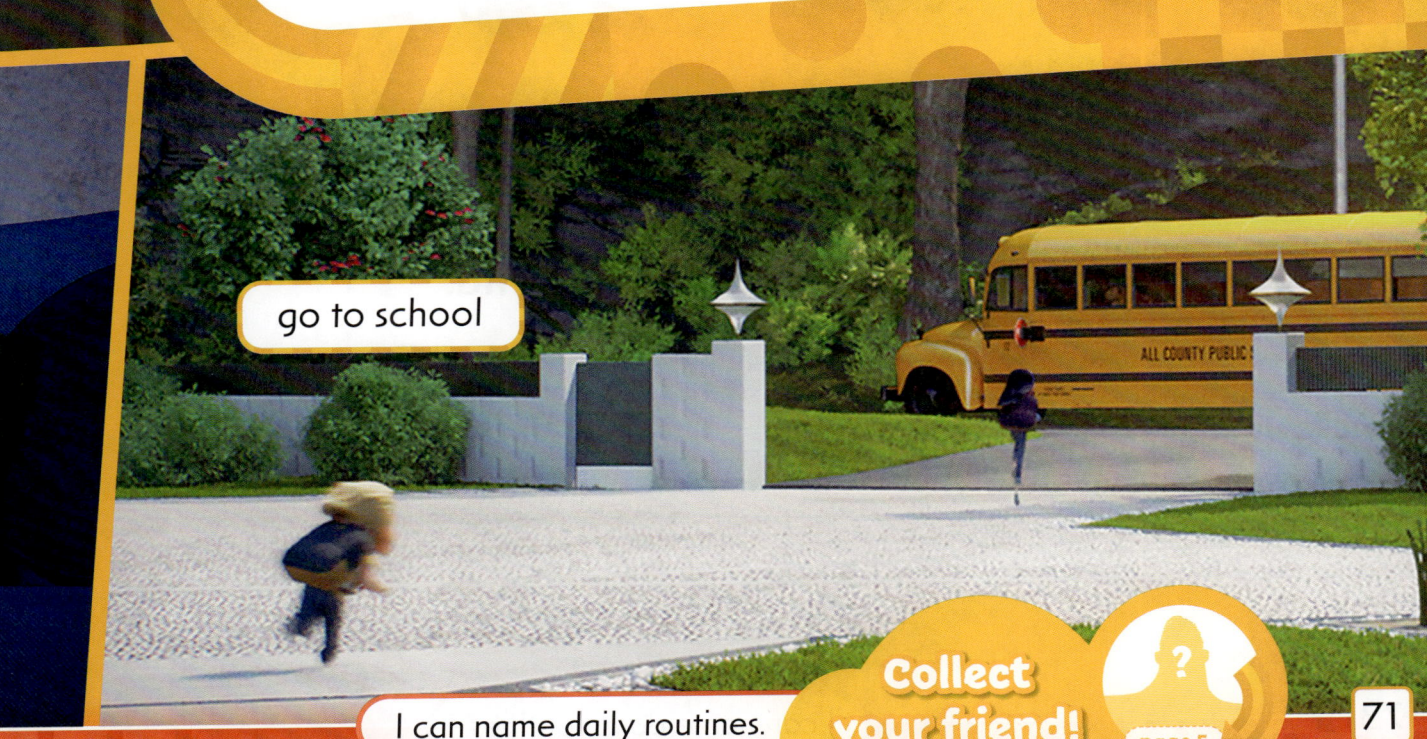

go to school

I can name daily routines.

Collect your friend!

LESSON 2
Vocabulary

1 🎧 6.3 💬 Listen, point, and say. Then play.

1. talk to my friends
2. come home 
3. exercise 
4. clean up 
5. pack my backpack 
6. wash my face 
7. go to sleep 
8. wake up 

2 🎧 6.4 ✏️ Listen and stick. Then circle.

Sticker time

1. I exercise / clean up.
2. I pack my backpack / go to sleep.
3. I wake up / wash my face.

3 ✏️ 💬 Write for you. Then tell a friend.

wake up ☀️ _____ _____ _____ go to sleep 💤

I wake up. Then I wash my face.

Talk buddies

I can name daily routines.

LESSON 3
Grammar

1 🎧 ✏️ **Listen and circle.**

They **talk to their friends** / **exercise** at school.

🎧 6.6
We watch TV every day.
They have dinner together.
Do you exercise?
Yes, we do./No, we don't.
Do they exercise?
Yes, they do./No, they don't.

2 🎧 **Listen and put a ✓ or ✗.**

	watch TV	cook dinner	talk to friends	exercise
Anna and her sister				
Mom and Dad				
me				

3 💬 **Look at 2. Put a ✓ or ✗ for you. Then ask and answer.**

Do you watch TV every day?

Yes, I do.

Talk buddies

I can ask and answer about daily routines.

LESSON 4 Story

Let's clean up!

1 🎧 6.8 Listen and read. Who reads a story to Oscar?

① Hi, Luiza. Can you come on Wednesday? I go to work at six o'clock.

And I come home at nine o'clock.

Yes, of course. See you then!

Thanks, Luiza!

② On Wednesday …

Do you want to watch TV with us, Amelia?

I can't. I have to do homework.

Would you like some of my chocolate, Amelia?

That's nice of you, Oscar.

③ Hey! Let's help Mom and Dad. Let's clean up the living room.

There's a lot to do!

④ We can all help. Then there isn't a lot to do.

Spot! Can you find Oscar's red shoes?

5 Oh, no! Look! It's eight-thirty. Oscar, wash your face. It's time for bed.

I can read you a story in bed. Come on!

6 At nine o'clock …

Wow! The house is so clean. Thank you, Luiza.

Thank you, Amelia and Oscar, too!

The end

2 Read and circle.

1. Mom and Dad go to **school** / **work**.
2. Oscar and Luiza **read a book** / **watch TV**.
3. Oscar goes to bed at **eight-thirty** / **nine o'clock**.
4. Amelia reads a story to **Oscar** / **her parents**.

3 Read and match. How do they help the family?

1. clean the house
2. read a story
3. go to work

a  b  c

4 Act out the story.

It's time for bed.

I can read you a story in bed.

Talk buddies

I can read and understand a story.

LESSON 5
Vocabulary

1 🎧 6.9 💬 **Listen, point, and say. Then play.**

1. in the morning
2. in the afternoon 
3. in the evening 
4. at night 
5. on the weekend 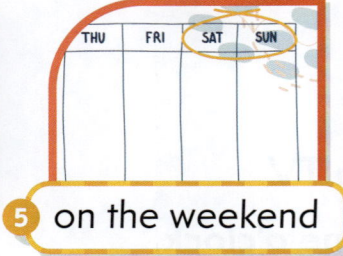
6. on Sundays 

Think and write.

the afternoon — in — spring
the morning

Picture Dictionary page 124

2 🎧 6.10 💬 **Listen and say. Then play in pairs.**

I go to sleep.
Yes!
At night.

Sing-along

3 🎵 6.11 **Listen, sing, and act.**

I wake up in the morning
And I go to school.
I do homework in the afternoon
And I clean up my room.

Every day is the same, work hard through the week.
On Monday to Friday, get up, go to sleep!

We have dinner in the evening,
Then I watch TV.
I go to bed at night
And I go to sleep.

Chorus

On the weekend it's different.
We have fun, fun, fun.
We go to the park
And play games in the sun, sun, sun!
We go to the park
And play games in the sun, sun, sun!

I can use simple time expressions.

Extra Lesson

Go online Phonics

LESSON 6
Grammar and Speaking

1 🎬 ✏️ Watch the video. Check (✓). When does Dash do his math homework?

in the morning ○   in the afternoon ○

🎧 6.12
When do you wake up?
I wake up in the morning.
I don't wake up at ten o'clock.

2 🎧 6.13 ✏️ Listen and circle. Then ask and answer.

💡 7:30 = seven-thirty

1	have breakfast	7:00 / 7:30
2	have lunch	12:30 / 1:00
3	do her homework	in the **afternoon** / **evening**
4	ride her bike	**on the weekend** / **on Mondays**

When do you have breakfast?

Let's communicate!

When do you wake up?

I wake up at 12:30 in the afternoon.

No!

3 💬 Use the cut outs. Play the game.

cut outs

I can ask and answer about daily routines.

77

LESSON 7
Myself and others

Helping at home

Listen and sing. 1.13

1 Look and say. How do they help the family?

2 Listen and number. How do they help at home?

a   b   c

3 How can you help at home? Write and tell a friend.

I can _____ .   That's nice.

Be a hero!
Make a list of things you can do to help at home.

Night and day

LESSON 8 — Science — **My world**

1 🎧 6.15 ✏️ **Let's explore!** Listen, read, and write.

Earth   Moon   Sun

We live on **Earth**. Earth is big and round. It **spins** around and it doesn't stop. It takes Earth 24 hours to spin around. 24 hours is one day and one night.

It's two o'clock in Mexico City. It's the afternoon and we can see the **Sun**. In Istanbul it's eleven o'clock and it's dark. It's the night and we can see the **Moon**.

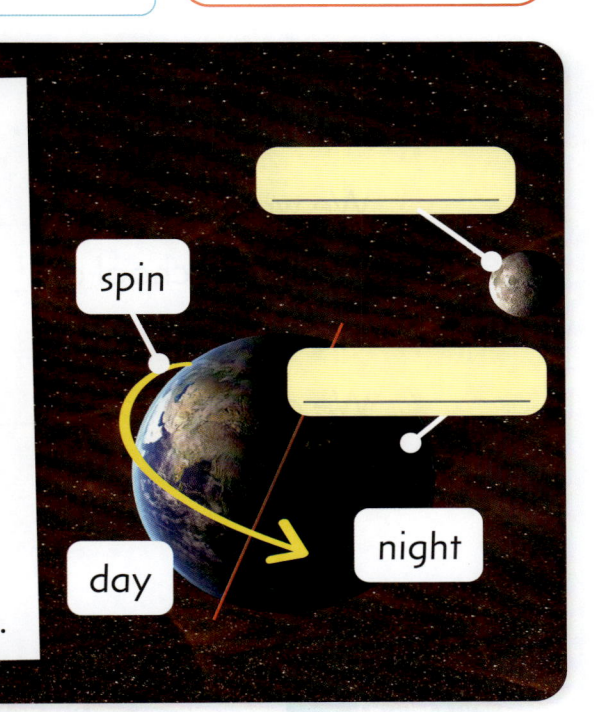

spin   day   night

2 💡 ✏️ **Think** Read and write *Yes* or *No*.

1. The Earth stops at night. _____
2. There are 24 hours in one day and night. _____
3. We can't see the Sun when it's dark. _____
4. We can see the Moon at night. _____

3 ✏️ **Do** When can you do this? Look and write *day*, *night*, or *both*.

1.   2.   3.   4.

I can read and understand about day and night.

LESSON 9
Project

My activities clock

Presentation

Let's review

1 🎧 6.16 ✏️ **Look, listen, and write.**

1. We wake up at _____.
2. We go to school at _____.
3. We come home at _____.
4. We go to sleep at _____.

Get ready

2 🎧 6.17 **Listen and check (✓). What does Lee do this time?**

- He speaks slowly. ◯
- He speaks fast. ◯
- He points at the clock. ◯
- He says the times. ◯

Workbook page 73

Create

3 🎨 💬 **Now make your activities clock. Then tell the class.**

Reflect 😞 🙂 😃

4 **How did I do?**

- I say the times. ◯
- I say what I do. ◯
- I point at the pictures. ◯
- I speak slowly. ◯

I can make and present an activities clock.

LESSON 10 Review

I can do it!

1 Look and write. Then listen and put a ✔ or ✘.

do homework
go to school
go to sleep
talk to friends

1. Do they _____ in the morning?
2. Do they _____ at school?
3. Do they _____ at night?
4. Do they _____ in the evening?

2 Look at 1. Ask and answer for you.

When do you do homework?

I do homework in the afternoon.

3 Think and check (✔). Then stick!

I can ...
- talk about daily routines and the time
- read a story
- sing a song
- help at home

Sticker time

✔ I completed Unit 6!

Go online
Big Project

81

7 At work

video-story

police officer

clerk

baker

LESSON 1 Vocabulary

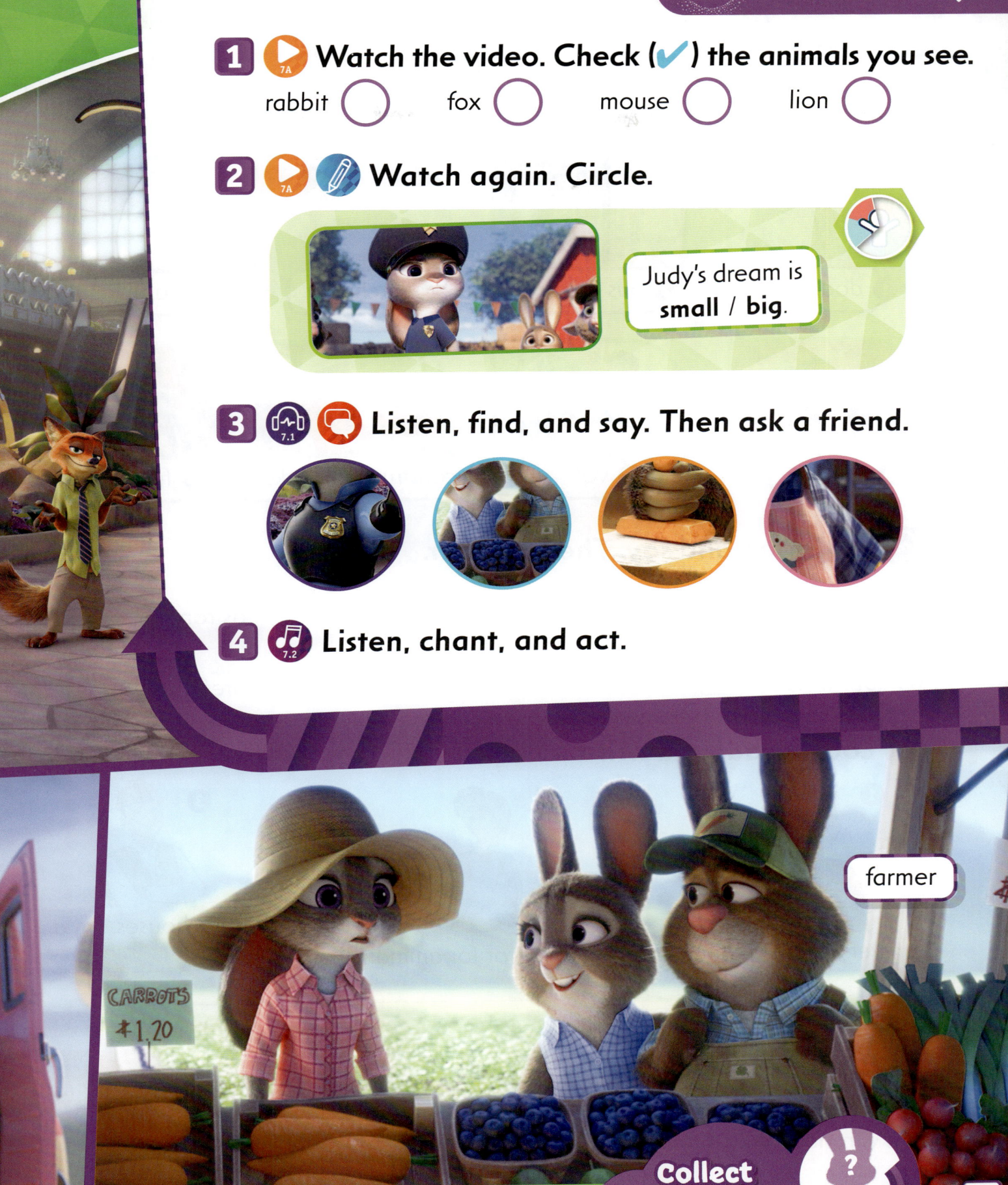

1 ▶ 7A Watch the video. Check (✓) the animals you see.

rabbit ◯   fox ◯   mouse ◯   lion ◯

2 ▶ 7A ✏️ Watch again. Circle.

Judy's dream is **small** / **big**.

3 🎧 7.1 💬 Listen, find, and say. Then ask a friend.

4 🎵 7.2 Listen, chant, and act.

farmer

I can name jobs.

Collect your friend! page 5

LESSON 2
Vocabulary

1 🎧 7.3 💬 Listen, point, and say. Then play.

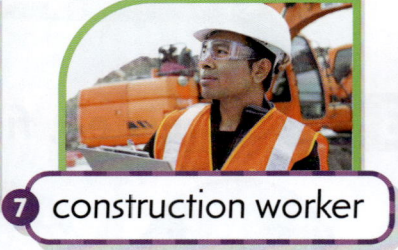

1. doctor
2. bus driver
3. architect
4. astronaut
5. athlete
6. vet
7. construction worker
8. firefighter

2 🎧 7.4 ✏️ Listen and say. Then number.

a. architect ___
b. doctor ___
c. astronaut ___
d. bus driver ___
e. vet ___
f. firefighter ___

3 ✏️ Look, read, and write.

1. I run very fast. I'm an _____.

2. I'm a doctor for animals. I'm a _____.

3. I build houses. I'm a _____.

4 💬 Play the game.

Astronaut.

Astronaut, construction worker.

Astronaut, construction worker, vet.

Talk buddies

I can name jobs.

LESSON 3
Grammar

1 🎧 ✏️ **Listen and circle.**

Judy wants to be a **firefighter** / **police officer**.

🎧 What do you want to be?
I want to be a baker.
She wants to be a police officer.
She doesn't want to be a farmer.

2 🎧 ✏️ **Listen and stick. Then circle.**

Sticker time

1. Nick **wants** / **doesn't want** to be a construction worker.

2. Nick **wants** / **doesn't want** to be a police officer.

3. Judy **wants** / **doesn't want** to be a farmer.

4. She **wants** / **doesn't want** to be an astronaut.

3 💬 **Play the game.**

What do you want to be?

I want to be a firefighter.

Amy wants to be a firefighter.

Talk buddies

I can ask and answer about jobs.

85

LESSON 4
Story

The firefighter

1 🎧 7.8 **Listen and read. What does Pedro want to be?**

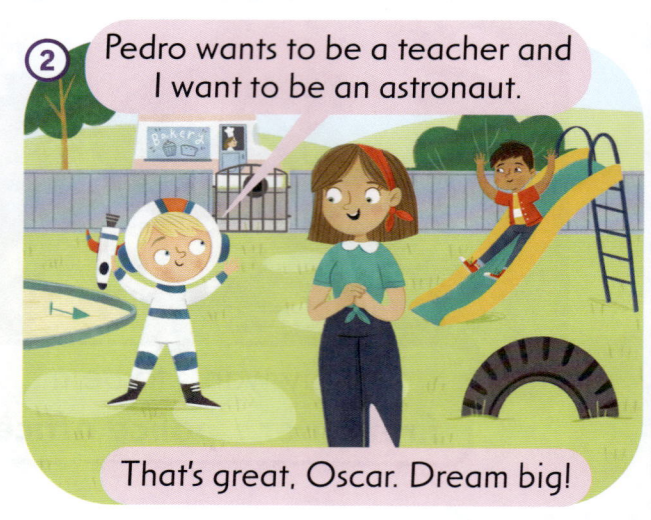

1. What do you want to be, Niko?
I want to be an athlete. What about you, Amelia?
I want to be a doctor.

2. Pedro wants to be a teacher and I want to be an astronaut.
That's great, Oscar. Dream big!

3. What does Laura want to be?
She wants to be a firefighter.

4. Can a girl be a firefighter, Laura?
Of course! I can show you a picture.

5. Oh, no! I can't find a picture of a firefighter, Niko.
Hmm … Come with me!

6. Look! There's a fire truck!
Ha ha! Yes. That's Aunt Rose.

Spot! Find a job beginning with the letter "b."

86

7 I want to be a firefighter, too.

Can I take a picture with you?

Fantastic! Dream big and work hard!

Yes, of course you can.

8 Great! I can add this to my book.

The end

2 Read and match.

1. Niko wants to be
2. Amelia wants to be
3. Oscar wants to be
4. Pedro wants to be
5. Laura wants to be

a. a teacher.
b. a firefighter.
c. an astronaut.
d. an athlete.
e. a doctor.

3 Circle. What do they say?

1. Dream **big** / **small**!
2. **Work** / **Play** hard!

4 Act out the story.

Look! There's a fire truck!

Ha ha! Yes.

Talk buddies

I can read and understand a story.

LESSON 5
Vocabulary

1 🎧 💬 Listen, point, and say. Then play.

1. drive
2. bake
3. design
4. build
5. rescue
6. teach

Think and group.

People or animals
rescue

Things
build

Picture Dictionary page 125

2 🎧 💬 Listen and say Yes or No. Then play in pairs.

Firefighters rescue vegetables.   No!

Sing-along

3 🎵 Listen, sing, and act.

What do you do? What do you do?
What do you do all day?

I teach children at school.
I design houses in the town.
I bake cookies and bread.

What do you do? What do you do?
What do you do all day?
Teach, design, bake bread?
What do you do all day?

I build apartment buildings in town.
I rescue people in my truck.
I drive a police car around.

What do you do? What do you do?
What do you do all day?
Build, drive, rescue people?
What do you do all day?

I can say what people do at work.

Extra Lesson

Go online
Phonics

88

LESSON 6
Grammar and Speaking

1 Watch the video. Circle. What does Gideon do?

7.12 What does she do?
She's a farmer. She grows vegetables.
She doesn't work at the police station.

2 Listen and say. Then match.

1. Emma
2. Malik
3. Belle
4. Stef

Let's communicate!

3 Use the cut outs. Play the game.

What does he do?

He helps animals. He's a vet.

I can ask and answer about people's jobs.

LESSON 7
Myself and others

Dreaming big

Listen and sing. 1.13

1 Look and say. What are their dreams?

2 Listen and circle. What's Cam's dream? Why is it hard? 7.14

I want to be **a teacher** / **an architect**.
It's hard because I can't **draw** / **paint**.

3 Choose and circle or think of your own ideas. Then write for you.

swim with sharks
drive a bus
build a house
design clothes
play soccer
be an astronaut
be a firefighter

My Dream

My name is _____.
My big dream is to _____
_____.
I can **work hard** / **dream big** / **do it!**

Be a hero!
It's OK to have small dreams, too. Make a list of your small dreams.

Self-awareness I can dream big.

Robots at work

LESSON 8
Technology — My world

1 🎧 **Let's explore!** Listen and read. Where can robots work?
7.15

Robots are **machines**. They help people do their jobs. Some robots are big and strong. They can **lift heavy** things and build houses.

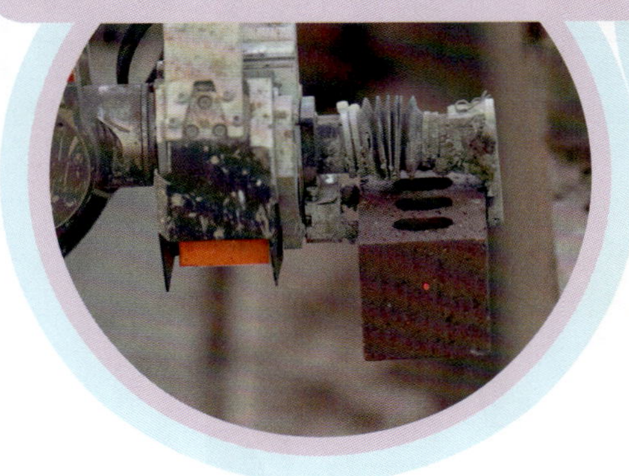

They can do **dangerous** jobs. They can work where people can't work: in the ocean or on the Moon.

Robots can work in factories, too. They can work during the day and at night. They don't feel tired or bored, and they can do the same job many times.

2 💡 **Think** Read and put a ✔ or ✘.

Same or different?	 👨‍🔬	 🤖
They can lift heavy things.		
They feel tired.		
They go to sleep at night.		
They can do dangerous jobs.		

3 ✏️ **Do** Write. How do these robots help people?

clean   cook   lift   make cars

1. 
2. 
3. 
4.

I can read and understand about how robots help people.

**LESSON 9
Project**

My dream job poster

self-management

Let's review

1 ✏️ **Look and write.**

① A _____ helps animals.

② A _____ works in a hospital.

Get ready

2 🎧 7.16 ✏️ **Listen and circle.**

Ollie wants to be a **farmer** / **clerk** / **vet**. He can **read a book** / **use a computer** / **talk to someone** to find out about his dream job.

Workbook page 85

Create

3 🎨 Now make your poster. Write.

Reflect ☹ 🙂 😃

4 How did I do?

I choose a job. ⭕

I find out about the job. ⭕

I make my poster. ⭕

I can make a poster about my dream job.

LESSON 10 Review

I can do it!

1 🎧 ✏️ **Listen and number.**

a   b   c   d

2 ✏️ **Read and write.**   design   drive   rescue   teach

1. A firefighter _____ people.
2. A teacher _____ at a school.
3. A bus driver _____ a bus.
4. An architect _____ houses.

3 💡 **Think and check (✓). Then stick!**

I can ...
- 💬 name jobs and say what people do ☐
- 📖 read a story ☐
- 🎵 sing a song ☐
- 🌈 work hard and dream big ☐

Sticker time

✅ I completed Unit 7!

Go online
Big Project

93

8 After school

video story

collect shells

buy ice cream

LESSON 1 Vocabulary

1 Watch the video. Check (✓). Where do Lilo and Stitch go?

park ○   beach ○   mall ○

2 Watch again. Circle.

Stitch is **nice** / **mean**.
Lilo is **sad** / **happy**.

3 Listen, find, and say. Then ask a friend.

4 Listen, chant, and act.

listen to music

go on a ride

I can name free-time activities.

Collect your friend! page 5

LESSON 2
Vocabulary

1 🎧 💬 Listen, point, and say. Then play.

1. do judo
2. surf the internet 
3. have a picnic 
4. go for a walk 
5. bowl 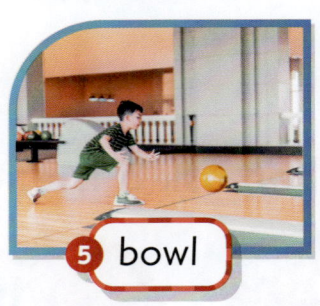
6. take a nap 
7. play table tennis 
8. do a jigsaw puzzle 

2 🎧 ✏️ Listen and stick. Then circle.

Sticker time

1. I have a picnic / take a nap.
2. I surf the internet / do a jigsaw puzzle.
3. We bowl / play table tennis.

3 💬 Ask and answer.

Do you do judo?
Yes, I do.

When do you do judo?
I do judo on Mondays.

Talk buddies

I can name free-time activities.

LESSON 3
Grammar

1 🎧 ✏️ **Listen and circle.**

Lilo and Stitch are **reading / taking a nap**.

🎧 8.6
They're reading a book.
They aren't taking a nap.
Are they listening to music?
Yes, they are./No, they aren't.

2 ✏️ 🎧 **Look, read, and write. Then listen and number.**

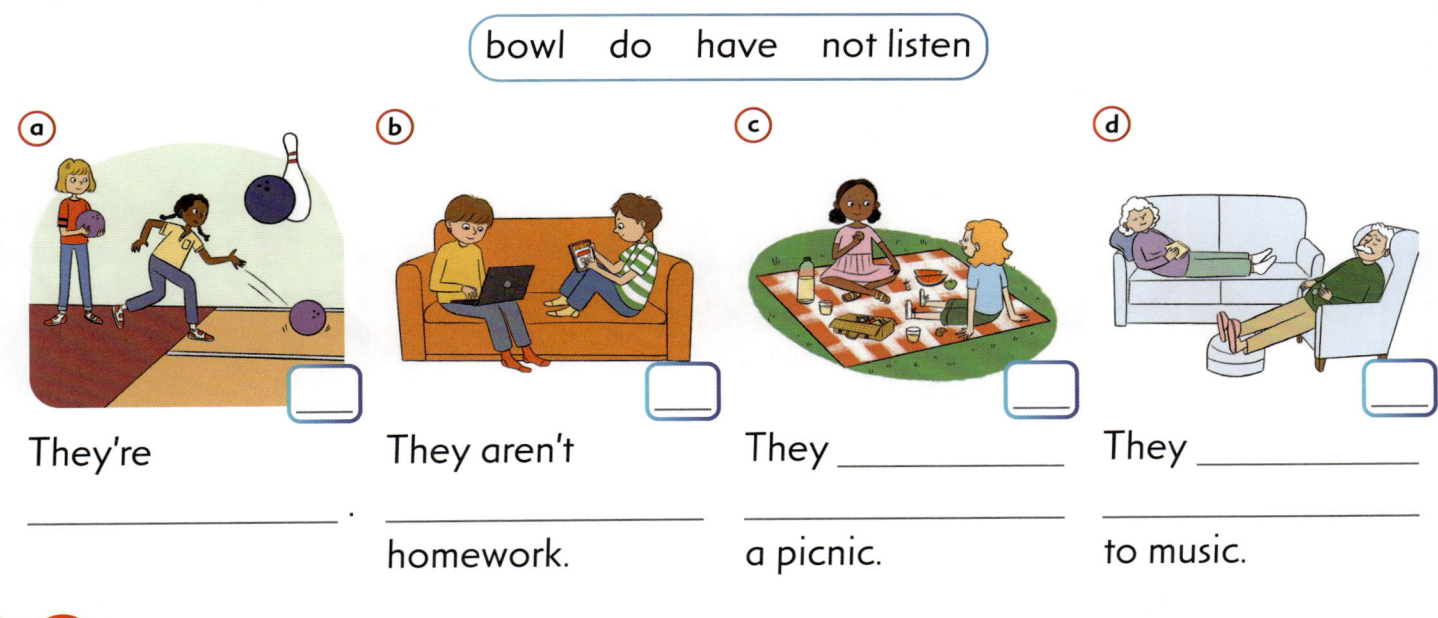

bowl   do   have   not listen

a) They're _____.

b) They aren't _____ homework.

c) They _____ a picnic.

d) They _____ to music.

3 💬 **Look at 2. Ask and answer**

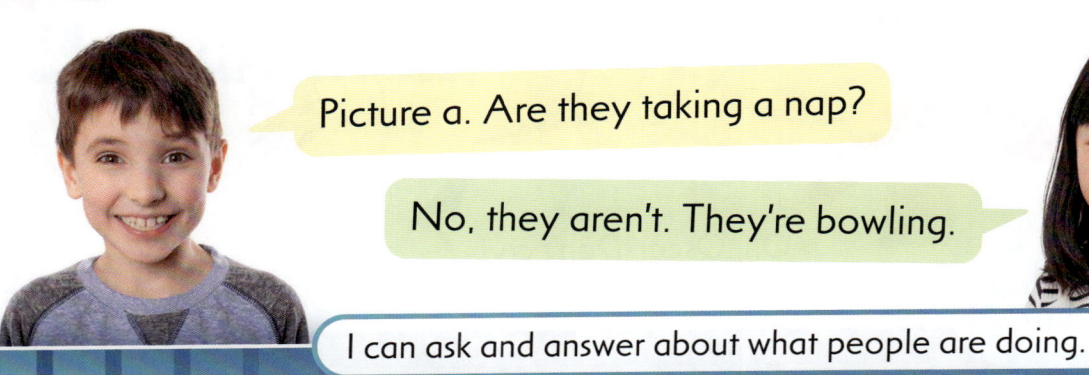

Picture a. Are they taking a nap?

No, they aren't. They're bowling.

Talk buddies

I can ask and answer about what people are doing.

97

LESSON 4
Story

The jigsaw puzzle

1 🎧 **Listen and read. Why is Oscar sad?**

1
- What are you doing, Amelia?
- I'm doing a jigsaw puzzle.
- Can I see?

2
- Yes, look! The kids are collecting shells and the man's buying ice cream.
- Oh, yes! And they're taking a nap.
- No, they're listening to music. Look!

3
- No, they're taking a nap!
- No, they aren't. Oh! Please let me do my puzzle!

4
- I don't like your puzzle!
- Oscar! No! Go away!

5
- You're mean, Amelia!
- Oh, Oscar. Don't cry!

6
- I'm sorry, Oscar. I feel bad, but you aren't helping me.

Spot! Can you find an ice cream?

7 I'm sorry, too. We can finish the jigsaw puzzle together.

Oh, thank you, Oscar. That's nice.

The end

2 Read and check (✓). What activities do you see?

- collect shells ○
- have a picnic ○
- do a jigsaw puzzle ○
- buy ice cream ○
- do judo ○
- listen to music ○

3 🖊 Read and circle. Then number.

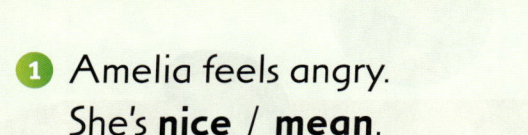

1. Amelia feels angry. She's **nice** / **mean**.
2. Oscar feels **happy** / **sad**.
3. Amelia feels **good** / **bad**. She's sorry.

a b c

4 💬 Act out the story.

Oh, yes! And they're taking a nap.

No, they're listening to music. Look!

Talk buddies

I can read and understand a story.

LESSON 5
Vocabulary

1 🎧 💬 **Listen, point, and say. Then play.**

1. play tag
2. kick a ball 
3. slide 
4. swing 
5. play hide and seek 
6. play in the playground 

Alone or with friends?

Alone
swing

With friends
play tag

Picture Dictionary
page 126

2 🎧 💬 **Listen and check (✔) in 1. Then play in pairs.**

Are you playing tag?

Sing-along

3 🎵 **Listen, sing, and act.**

Do you want to play in the playground with me?
We can kick a ball.
We can slide and we can swing.

Do you want to play in the playground with me?
Close your eyes.
Let's play hide and seek.

Do you want to play in the playground today?
We can play tag.
Quick! Run away!

I can name playground activities.

Extra Lesson >>>>>>>

Go online
Phonics

LESSON 6
Grammar and Speaking

1 Watch the video. Circle. Who's rescuing Lilo?

He's playing hide and seek.
She isn't swinging.
Is he sliding?   Yes, he is./No, he isn't.

2 Look and write Yes or No. Then cover and tell a friend.

A boy is swinging.

1. A boy is kicking a ball. _____
2. A girl is sliding. _____
3. A boy is swinging. _____
4. Two boys are playing tag. _____
5. A girl is taking a nap. _____

Let's communicate!

3 Use the cut outs. Play the game.

Is Amy sliding?

No, she isn't.

I can ask and answer about what people are doing.

LESSON 7
Myself and others

Noticing effects of behavior

Listen and sing. 🎵 1.13

1 💬 Look and say. Who's mean? Who feels sad?

2 🎧 Look, listen, and check (✓). 8.13

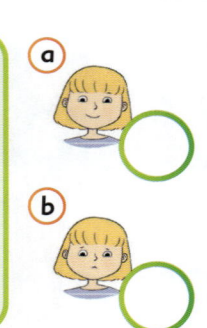

1. Go away!
   a
   b

2. I can help you.
   a
   b

3 💡 ✏️ Read and draw 🙂 or ☹️.

My action	My friend feels …
I share my ice cream.	→
I ask you to play.	→
I kick.	→

⭐ Be a hero! ⭐
Do you feel bad about something? Make a card to say "I'm sorry."

I'm sorry!

Relationship skills I can notice how my behavior affects others.

How things fly

LESSON 8
My world — Engineering

1 🎧 **Let's explore!** Listen and read. What does a plane need to fly?

Birds have **wings**. They use their muscles to move their wings up and down. Air **pressure** lifts them up.

wing
pressure
engine
air

Planes have wings, too. But they don't move up and down. Planes have **engines**. They move the plane forward. The **air** moves over and under the wings. The air pressure over the plane is different from the air pressure under the plane. The air pressure helps lift the plane up.

2 💡 **Think** Read and put a ✔ or ✘.

	moves its wings	has engines	uses air pressure	can fly
a bird				
a plane				

3 ✏️ **Do** How does it fly? Look and write *wings* or *engine*.

1. 2. 3. 4.

_____   _____   _____   _____

I can read and understand about how things fly.

103

LESSON 9
Project

My free time poster

Presentation

Let's review

1 🎧 8.15 ✏️ **Listen and number in order. Then match.**

- I'm playing with my friends.
- (a) I'm collecting leaves.
- (b) Millie's swinging
- (c) Kevin's kicking his ball.

Get ready

2 🎧 8.16 **Listen and check (✓).**

Workbook page 97

Create

3 🎨 💬 **Now make your poster. Then tell the class.**

Reflect ☹️ 🙂 😃

4 How did I do?

- I make my project. ⭕
- I practice my presentation. ⭕
- I present my poster. ⭕

I can make and present a poster about my free-time activities.

**LESSON 10
Review**

I can do it!

1 🎧 ✏️ **Listen and number. Then play.**

Take a nap. One!

a b c d e f

2 ✏️ **Look, read, and write.**

1. Is Lilo singing? _____
2. Are they dancing? _____

3. _____ Stitch _____ the guitar?
4. _____

3 💡 **Think and check (✓). Then stick!**

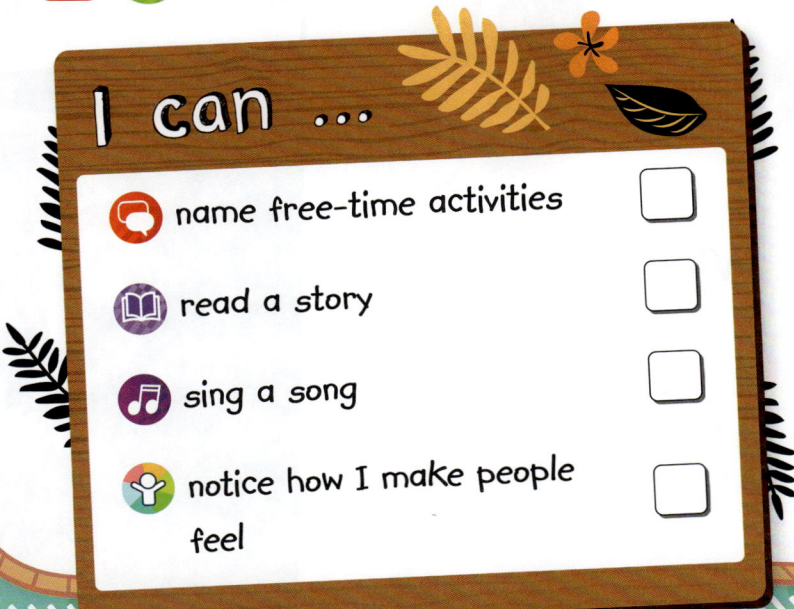

I can ...
- 💬 name free-time activities ☐
- 📖 read a story ☐
- 🎵 sing a song ☐
- 🙋 notice how I make people feel ☐

Sticker time

✓ I completed Unit 8!

Go online
Big Project

105

9 Party time

decorations

1 Watch the video. Check (✓). Who's the party for?

2 Watch again. Write. What's the problem?

_____ isn't helping. He's eating the _____.

LESSON 1 **Vocabulary**

3 🎧 9.1 💬 Listen, find, and say. Then ask a friend.

4 🎵 9.2 Listen, chant, and act.

video story

banner

birthday cake

balloons

I can name party things.

Collect your friend! page 5

107

LESSON 2
Vocabulary

1 🎧 9.3 💬 Listen, point, and say. Then play.

1. decorate a cake
2. give a gift 
3. blow out candles 
4. put up decorations 
5. make a card 
6. invite friends 
7. blow up balloons 
8. make goody bags 

2 🎧 9.4 ✏️ Listen and stick. Then circle.

Sticker time

1. Mom is **decorating a cake** / **making a card**.
2. Ava is **giving a gift** / **making goody bags**.
3. Pablo is **blowing out candles** / **blowing up balloons**.

3 💬 What does your family do for your birthday party? Tell a friend.

My mom decorates a cake.

I put up decorations.

Talk buddies

I can talk about party preparations.

LESSON 3
Grammar

1 🎧 ✏️ **Listen and circle.**

What are you doing?
I'm reading.
What's Anna doing?
She's listening.
What are they doing?
They're singing.

They're **reading books** / **singing**.

2 🎧 ✏️ **Listen and number.**

1. Jenny
2. Will
3. Kate
4. Jon

3 💬 **Look at 2. Play Guess who?**

What are you doing?
You're Jon!

I'm decorating a cake.

Talk buddies

I can ask and answer about what people are doing.

109

Lesson 4
Story

The party

1 🎧 9.8 **Listen and read. Who's the party for?**

1
— Hi, Niko! Are you getting ready for the party?
— Yes, we are. I'm decorating the cake. Come in.

2
— Dad's in charge.
— We still have to decorate the cake, clean the yard, and put up decorations!
— Don't worry. We can help.

3
— What are Amelia and Oscar doing?
— They're cleaning the yard and blowing up balloons.
— What's Laura doing?
— She's making a banner.

4
— Hey, Pedro! Can you help put up the decorations?
— Yes, of course. Let's work together.

5
— Quick! Luiza comes home at six o'clock.

Spot! Can you find a gift?

6 At six o'clock …

Wow! Thank you, Niko!

Thank you!

It's from *all* of us, Luiza!

GOODBYE LUIZA!

The end

2 Check (✔) and say. What are they doing?

decorating a cake					
making a banner					
putting up decorations					
blowing up balloons					
cleaning the yard					

3 Read, write, and check (✔).

1. Who's in charge?
   _____

2. How many jobs are there?
   _____

3. What does Niko help with?
   a  b  c

4 Act out the story.

Wow! Thank you!

It's from *all* of us!

Talk buddies

I can read and understand a story.

LESSON 5
Vocabulary

1 🎧 9.9 💬 Listen, point, and say. Then play.

1. watermelon
2. popcorn
3. party hat
4. mask
5. lemonade
6. candy

Make your own picture dictionary.

party hat

Picture Dictionary
page 127

2 🎧 9.10 💬 Listen and check (✓) in 1. Then tell a friend.

For my party, I have popcorn and watermelons.

Sing-along

3 🎵 9.11 Listen, sing, and act.

Popcorn, watermelons, lemonade, and candy.
I'm getting ready for my party!

I'm wearing a mask.
I'm a black and white cat.
And on my head,
There's a green party hat.

Chorus

We're making popcorn
And eating cake.
Let's blow out the candles:
Six, seven, eight!

Chorus

I can name party things.

Extra Lesson

Go online
Phonics

LESSON 6
Grammar and Speaking

1 Watch the video. Circle Anna's gifts.

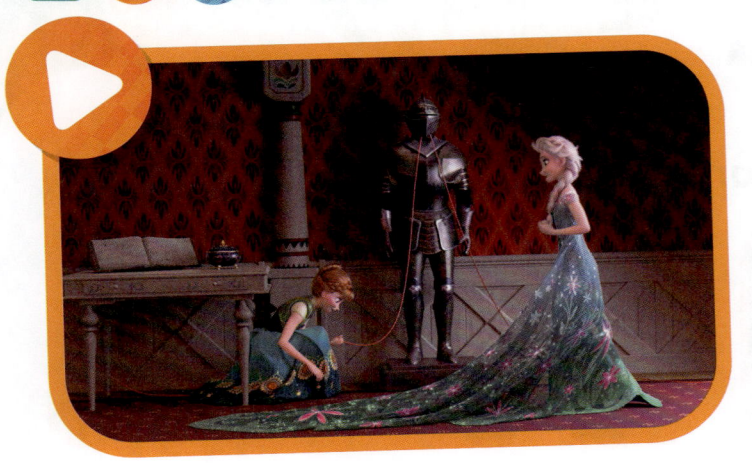

It's Anna's dress.
They're Lucas's books.

2 Follow and find. Then ask and answer.

① Vicky ② Carlos ③ Cody ④ Ali

What are these?

They're Ali's gifts.

a 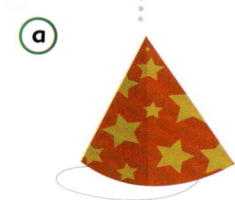 b  c  d

Let's communicate!

It's Jun's plane.

They're Nathan's books.

3 Use the cut outs. Play the game.

cut outs

I can say who things belong to.

113

LESSON 7
Myself and others

Sharing tasks

Listen and sing. 1.13

1 🗨 Look and say. Who's in charge? Who helps?

2 🎧✏️ Listen and circle.
   ① They're making **party hats** / **masks**.
   ② **Tom** / **Emily** is in charge.

3 💡✏️ Look and draw. How can they share the tasks?

Be a hero!
Are your friends getting ready for something? Is it a big job? Ask how you can help them.

Responsible decision-making I can share tasks in a team.

Rosemaling patterns

LESSON 8
My world — Art

1 🎧 **Let's explore!** Listen and read.
What do you need to make Rosemaling art?

This colorful **pattern** is an example of Rosemaling art. There are a lot of flowers, circles, and lines. You make them with a **paintbrush**. You can put two colors on the paintbrush at the same time.

The patterns are the same on each side of the picture. This is called **symmetry**. To make a pattern, repeat the same shape many times.

- pattern
- paintbrush
- symmetry
- curvy line

To make a flower, paint a **curvy** line, a little like a "C" shape. Then paint another "C" shape across from it. Between them, paint an "S" shape.

2 💡 **Think** Read and circle.

1. You make Rosemaling art with **a paintbrush** / **your fingers**.
2. You can put **two** / **three** colors on the paintbrush.
3. Rosemaling art uses a lot of **black** / **curvy** lines.
4. To make a **flower** / **leaf** you paint two "C" shapes.

3 ✏️ **Do** Look and finish the pattern.

I can read and understand about patterns.

LESSON 9
Project

My cake design

Let's review

1 Read and circle. Which cake is for May?

May's favorite color is green, so the cake is green. She doesn't like flowers. She likes balloons. May's seven, so there are seven balloons on the cake.

Get ready

2 Look and check (✓). Who's ready to work?

Workbook page 109

Create

3 Now design your cake. Write.

Reflect

4 How did I do?

- I know what to do.
- I ask for help if I need it.
- I make my project.
- I do my best.

I can design and describe a birthday cake.

LESSON 10 Review

I can do it!

1 Circle and say. What are they doing?

1. He's **baking** / **making** a card
2. They're blowing **up** / **out** balloons 
3. He's **putting up** / **giving** a gift 
4. He's **inviting** / **decorating** a cake 

2 Look and write.

1. they / Olaf / friends _____
2. they / run _____
3. it / Kristoff / paintbrush _____ 
4. they / make / a banner _____

3 Think and check (✓). Then stick!

I can ...
- 💬 talk about parties ⚪
- 📖 read a story ⚪
- 🎵 sing a song ⚪
- 🧑 help others and share tasks ⚪

Test your progress with English Benchmark Young Learners

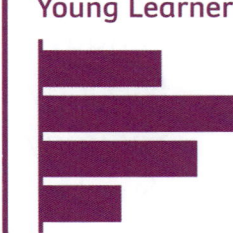

sticker time

✓ I completed Unit 9!

Go online Big Project

117

W 1 Find and stick. 2 🎧 Listen, point, and say. 3 ✏️ Write.

Sticker time

a hundred   eighty   fifty   forty   ninety   seventy   sixty   thirty   twenty

20 ____   30 ____   40 ____   [ ] ____   60 ____

70 ____   [ ] ____   90 ____   100 ____

Friday
~~Monday~~
Saturday
Sunday
Thursday
Tuesday
Wednesday

Monday
1   2 ____   3 ____   4 ____

5 ____   6 ____   7 ____

1

1 Find and stick.   **2** 🎧 10.2 Listen, point, and say.   **3** ✏️ Write.
4 Think and draw.

fast   short
strong   tall

beard   blond   curly
dark   glasses
gray   long   straight

have

cook   horseback ride
play basketball
play the drums
ride a scooter   take pictures

119

2

1 Find and stick. **2** 🎧 10.3 Listen, point, and say. **3** ✏️ Write.
4 Animals or things? Write.

boat   ocean
octopus   shark

beach   crab
dolphin   jellyfish
sea lion   shell
starfish   whale

bucket   sandcastle   sunhat
surfboard   towel   umbrella

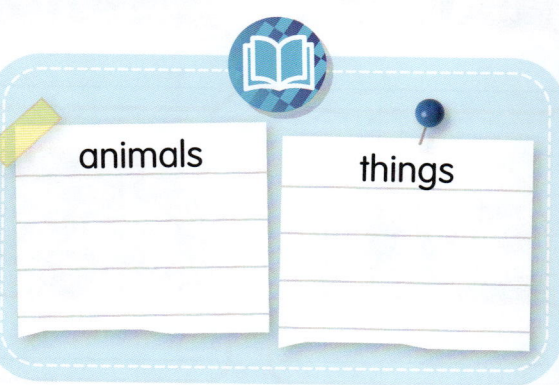

animals	things

3

1 Find and stick. **2** 🎧 Listen, point, and say. **3** ✏️ Write.
4 Circle the odd one out.

Sticker time

bus street
tram truck

bookstore fire station
grocery store hospital
movie theater
museum restaurant
train station

📖

1 factory hotel
  fire station
2 movie theater
  museum
  hospital
3 mall
  sports center
  grocery store

apartment building
factory hotel mall
police station
sports center

121

4

1. Find and stick. 2. 🎧 Listen, point, and say. 3. ✏️ Write.
4. What food do you eat?

cake   peas   potatoes   soup

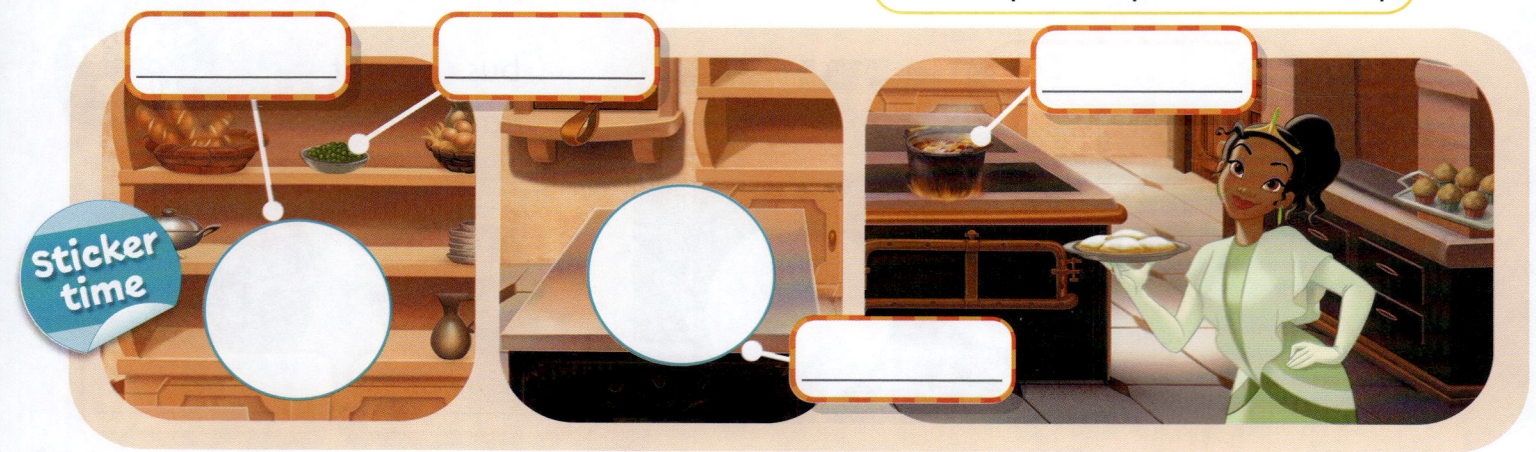

Sticker time

chicken   chocolate
kiwis   lemons
mangoes   nuts
pineapples   yogurt

breakfast   burger   cereal
dinner   fries   lunch

breakfast   lunch   dinner

122

5

1 Find and stick.   **2** 🎧 Listen, point, and say.   **3** ✏️ Write.
4 What can you do?

fall   spring   summer   winter

cloudy   cool   rainy
snowy   stormy
sunny   warm   windy

☀️ It's hot.

❄️ It's cold.

fly a kite   go sledding
go to the park
make snowballs
plant seeds   play indoors

6

1 Find and stick.   **2** 🎧 Listen, point, and say.   **3** ✏️ Write.
4 In, on, or at?

do homework   go to school   go to work   watch TV

come home   clean up   exercise   go to sleep
pack my backpack   talk to my friends   wake up   wash my face

at night   in the afternoon
in the evening   in the morning
on Sundays   on the weekend

in   on   at

7

1 Find and stick.   **2** 🎧 Listen, point, and say.   **3** ✏️ Write.
4 Think and group.

baker   clerk   farmer   police officer

Sticker time

architect   astronaut   athlete   bus driver   construction worker
doctor   firefighter   vet

| help/rescue | design/make |

bake   build   design
drive   rescue   teach

8

1 Find and stick.   **2** 🎧 Listen, point, and say.   **3** ✏️ Write.
4 Circle activities you do at home. Then write two more.

buy ice cream   collect shells
go on a ride   listen to music

Sticker time

bowl   do a jigsaw puzzle   do judo   go for a walk   have a picnic
play table tennis   surf the internet   take a nap

kick a ball   play hide and seek
play in the playground
play tag   slide   swing

9

1 Find and stick. **2** 🎧 Listen, point, and say. **3** ✏️ Write.
4 Circle things for your party. Then draw one more.

balloons   banner
birthday cake   decorations

Sticker time

blow out candles   blow up balloons   decorate a cake   give a gift
invite friends   make a card   make goody bags   put up decorations

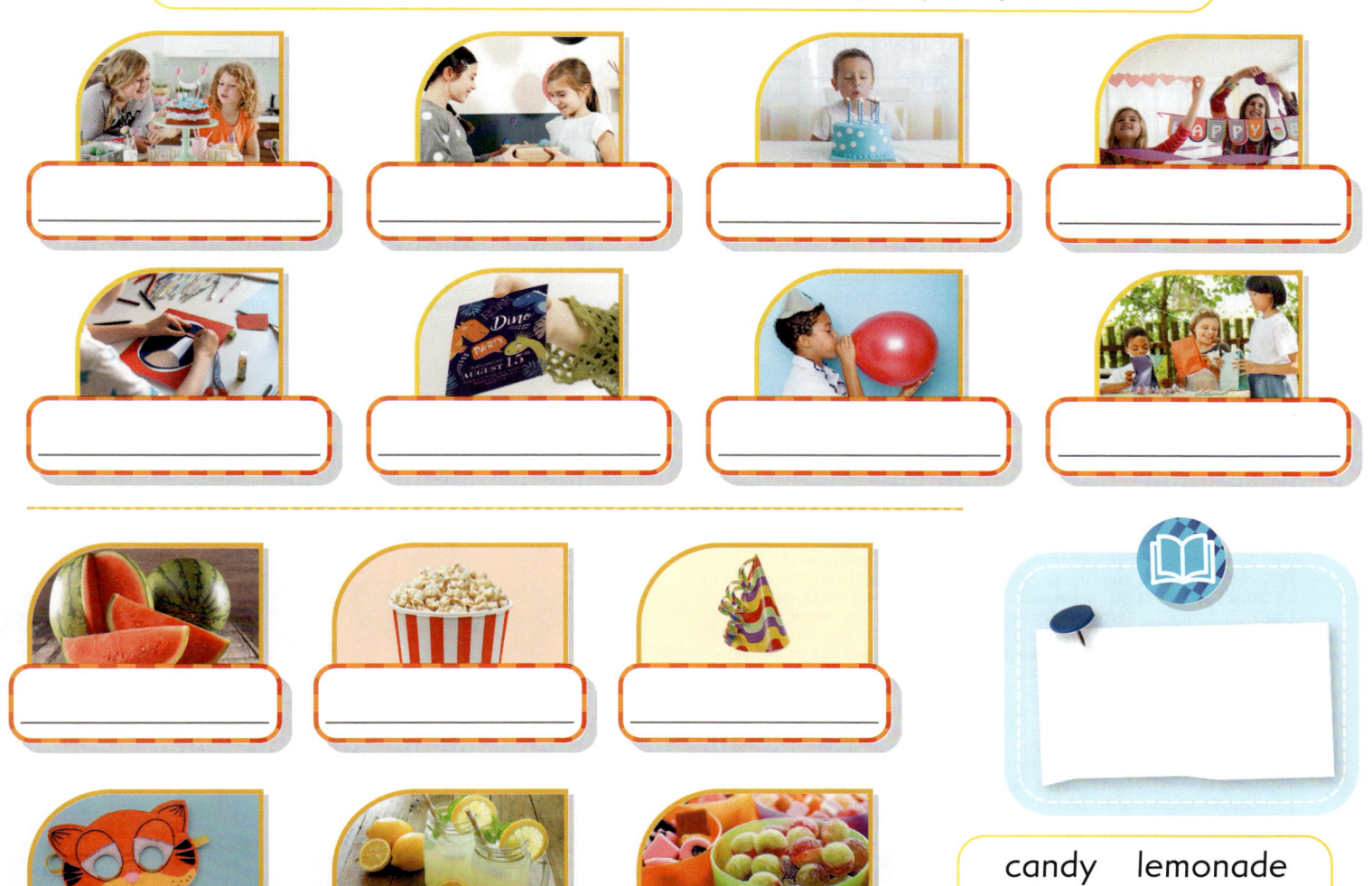

candy   lemonade
mask   party hat
popcorn   watermelon

127

Pearson Education Limited
KAO Two
KAO Park
Hockham Way
Harlow, Essex
CM17 9SR
England
and Associated Companies throughout the world.

pearsonenglish.com
© Pearson Education Limited 2022

© 2022 Disney Enterprises, Inc. All rights reserved. Pixar properties © Disney/Pixar

The movie THE PRINCESS AND THE FROG Copyright © 2009 Disney, story inspired in part by the book THE FROG PRINCESS by E.D. Baker Copyright © 2002, published by Bloomsbury Publishing, Inc.

The right of Cheryl Pelteret and Viv Lambert to be identified as authors of this Work has been asserted by them in accordance with the Copyright, Designs and Patents Act 1988.

All rights reserved; no part of this publication may be reproduced, stored in a retrieval system, or transmitted in any form or by any means, electronic, mechanical, photocopying, recording, or otherwise without the prior written permission of the Publishers.

First published 2022
ISBN: 978-1-292-44157-3
Set in Arta Medium 19/25pt

Printed in Slovakia by Neografia

Acknowledgements

The publishers and authors would like to thank the following people for their feedback and comments during the development of the material: Dilek Akin, Burcu Hasbay, Martha Illescas, Maja Jankovic, Sandy Meza, Monica Medina, Olga Mokrushina, Soledad O'Keefe, Anita Parlaj.

Image Credits

123RF.com: Arcady31 18, Atoss 48, Belchonock 48, Cathy Yeulet 92, 100, Choreograph 52, Chuyu 60, Dolgachov 5, HONGQI ZHANG 51, Iakov Filimonov 100, IKO 12, Insidecreativehouse 39, Inspirestock International - Exclusive Contributor 108, Jackf 88, Joshua Resnick 52, Kittipong Jirasukhanont 91, Lipik 12, Margouillat 112, Mcherevan 48, Michael Gray 56, Mongkol Chakritthakool 67, Nilanjan Bhattacharya 18, Romrodinka 53, Saksit054 96, Sergey Dzyuba 35, Soleg 35, Srapulsar38 18, Stylephotographs 108, Tinna2727 72, Tobi 52, Ximagination 16; **Alamy Stock Photo:** Cultura RM 96, Design Pics 93, Evan Sklar 41, FOODLOVE 36, Geogphotos 43, Inga Spence 48, Kasefoto 112, Kian Khoon Tan 18, LJSphotography 111, Lumi Images 108, Murat Tegmen 28, Nature Picture Library 31, Olaf Schuelke 43, SD 75, Susan Fisher Plotner-VIEW 36, T.M.O.Buildings 40, WaterFrame 24; **Getty Images:** Aleksandra Alekseeva 76, Alexey_Fedoren 76, Anastasia Dobrusina 108, AndreaObzerova 111, Ariel Skelley 64, Artit Wongpradu / EyeEm 78, Asia Images Group 73, BananaStock 104, Beyhanyazar 92, Blue Images 53, Brand X Pictures 36, BrianLasenby 31, Christopher Hopefitch 54, Clicksbyabrar 28, DarioGaona 57, Diego Fiore 43, Emma Kim 12, EMS-FORSTER-PRODUCTIONS 108, Erstudiostok 32, Flashpop 99, Fotokostic 96, Fundamental rights 96, Fuse 78, Geber86 16, George Doyle 40, GlobalStock 32, GrapeImages 64, Guaraciaba Ferreira / EyeEm 53, Herraez 84, Image Source 72, Imagesbybarbara 68, Imgorthand 64, 96, Ines Carrara 103, Izusek 16, J-Elgaard 36, Jamie Grill 100, 108, JBryson 40, 101, JGI/Daniel Grill 100, JGI/Tom Grill 79, Jose Luis Pelaez Inc 93, 112, Kelvin Murray 72, Kenishirotie 96, Kimberrywood 20, Klaus Vedfelt 76, Lane Oatey / Blue Jean Images 16, Lathuric 113, Leland Bobbe 12, 57, LittleBee80 64, Lumi Images/Dario Secen 100, LumineImages 54, LWA/Dann Tardif 53, Maskot 40, MBI 72, 76, 88, MediaProduction 91, Michelle McMahon 112, Momcilog 65, Nattrass 72, Obradovic 42, Paul Biris 64, Paul Brown 35, PeakSTOCK 101, Plan Shoot / Multi-bits 90, Pookpiik 100, Rani Sr Prasiththi / EyeEm 29, Ridofranz 72, S_Bachstroem 91, Scorpion26 28, SDI Productions 88, SergiyN 27, Shank_ali 40, Shoo_arts 115, Skodonnell 84, Skynesher 116, SStajic 28, Stefka Pavlova 108, Steve Prezant 16, Swyz 72, The Good Brigade 48, Tomas Ragina 60, 60, Tuan Tran 89, Wavebreakmedia 93, 116, Yongyuan 96, Zenstock 40, Zing Images 12; **Hako Machines Ltd:** 91; **Pearson Education Ltd:** Alice McBroom 44, 44, Jon Barlow 42, 51, 52, Studio 8 65, Trevor Clifford 28, Tudor Photography 64, 78; **Shutterstock:** 5 second Studio 48, Aaron Amat 16, Africa Studio 57, 84, Ahmad Ihsan 27, Aksinia Abiagam 29, Albert Pego 24, Alberto Zamorano 36, Aleksandrova Karina 52, Alena Ozerova 12, 96, Alex Coan 57, AlexeyNikitin1981 18, Alexkar08 60, Alvaro Tejero 87, Amelia Martin 67, Andrea Izzotti 24, Anna Nahabed 109, Anoly_Di 89, Anton Albert 48, Arakelyan Andrey 109, Asier Romero 17, BigMouse 43, Brian A Jackson 54, Cedric Weber 36, Chris Briggs 88, Christian Jung 57, Cre8tive Images 57, Cristian Zamfir 43, Cristovao 30, David Zalubowski/AP/Shutterstock 91, Decha Laoharuengrongkun 16, Deyan Georgiev 63, Dionisvera 57, Djomas 52, 60, Dmitry Kalinovsky 88, Elena Nichizhenova 76, Elena Schweitzer 112, FamVeld 60, Ferenc Szelepcsenyi 40, FloridaStock 103, FREEPIK2 87, George Rudy 36, Gino Santa Maria 116, Grand Warszawski 40, Hafakot 37, Henk Bouma 67, Inate 18, Jeka 100, JeniFoto 112, Jenson 91, Johnfoto18 57, Julia Sudnitskaya 48, Juver 76, 112, Kameel4u 64, Kaspars Grinvalds 84, Kenishirotie 79, Kerimli 24, Khosro 12, Kinga 17, Konstantin Novikov 31, Krakenimages.com 16, Ladybirdstudio 76, LightField Studios 72, Littlekidmoment 37, 75, LiuSol 97, Lovepaul2558 28, M. Unal Ozmen 112, MAHATHIR MOHD YASIN 52, MaraZe 48, 57, Marko Aliaksandr 88, Marozau Andrei 67, Martin Bergsma 18, Maryna Kulchytska 113, Max Dallocco 76, MBI 52, 52, 60, 77, 84, Michaeljung 99, Mikbiz 35, Mircea BEZERGHEANU 24, Muratart 103, Mykhaylo Palinchak 79, Nattika 57, Ndoeljindoel 84, Netfalls Remy Musser 42, Nikola Bilic 24, Palmer Kane LLC 100, Patrick Rolands 24, Paulaphoto 16, Photos BrianScantlebury 24, Pixel-Shot 79, PMN PHOTO 57, Prostock-studio 84, Ramona Heim 60, Rawpixel.com 53, RedKoala 115, Robert Kneschke 93, Rostislav Stefanek 67, Rozochkalvn 48, 76, rSnapshotPhotos 41, 76, Ryszard Filipowicz 28, S-F 54, Sanneberg 56, Sashahaltam 80, Sateesh Lacheta 67, Schankz 67, Sebikus 79, Sergey Nivens 103, Serhii Bobyk 36, Silberkorn 48, Sirikorn Thamniyom 15, Studioloco 63, 114, Sunabesyou 73, Suwin 91, Svtdesign 91, Sweet_Cheeks 108, Syda Productions 100, T.TATSU 97, Terry Reimink 103, Tom Wang 102, TY Lim 66, 78, Vadim Orlov 60, VAKS-Stock Agency 84, VALUA STUDIO 39, VanderWolf Images 40, Veronica Louro 15, 88, Vibrant Image Studio 60, Vladimir Wrangel 31, Wavebreakmedia 77, Yongkiet jitwattanatam 67, Zarnell Photography 103, Zurijeta 12, Zwiebackesser 90.

Cover images © 2022 Disney Enterprises, Inc. All rights reserved. Pixar properties © Disney/Pixar

Illustrations

Anna Bishop/Advocate: pp.42, 49, 78, 96, 97, 101 (activity 2), 102, 104 (activity 2), 105, 117; **Martyn Cain/Beehive Illustration:** pp.17, 29 (activity 3), 41 (activity 1), 53 (activity 3), 65, 77, 89, 101 (activity 3), 113 (activity 2); **Emily Cooksey/Plum Pudding:** pp.20, 32, 44, 56, 64, 92, 104 (activity 1), 114 (party hats only), 116; **Samara Hardy/Plum Pudding:** (course characters); **Jo Parry/Advocate:** pp.60, 61, 67, 68, 69; **Adriana Puglisi/Plum Pudding:** (doodles), pp.65, 66, 72, 108; **Nez Riaz/Advocate:** p.55; **Sean Simms/Advocate:** pp.8, 16, 21, 24, 25, 28, 29 (activity 2), 30, 46, 52, 54, 113 (activity 1), 114 (activity 3); **Diego Vaisberg/Advocate:** pp.25, 33, 36, 37, 41 (activity 2), 43, 45, 48, 53 (activity 2), 79, 80, 115; **Steven Wood/Advocate:** pp.18, 19.

Cut outs

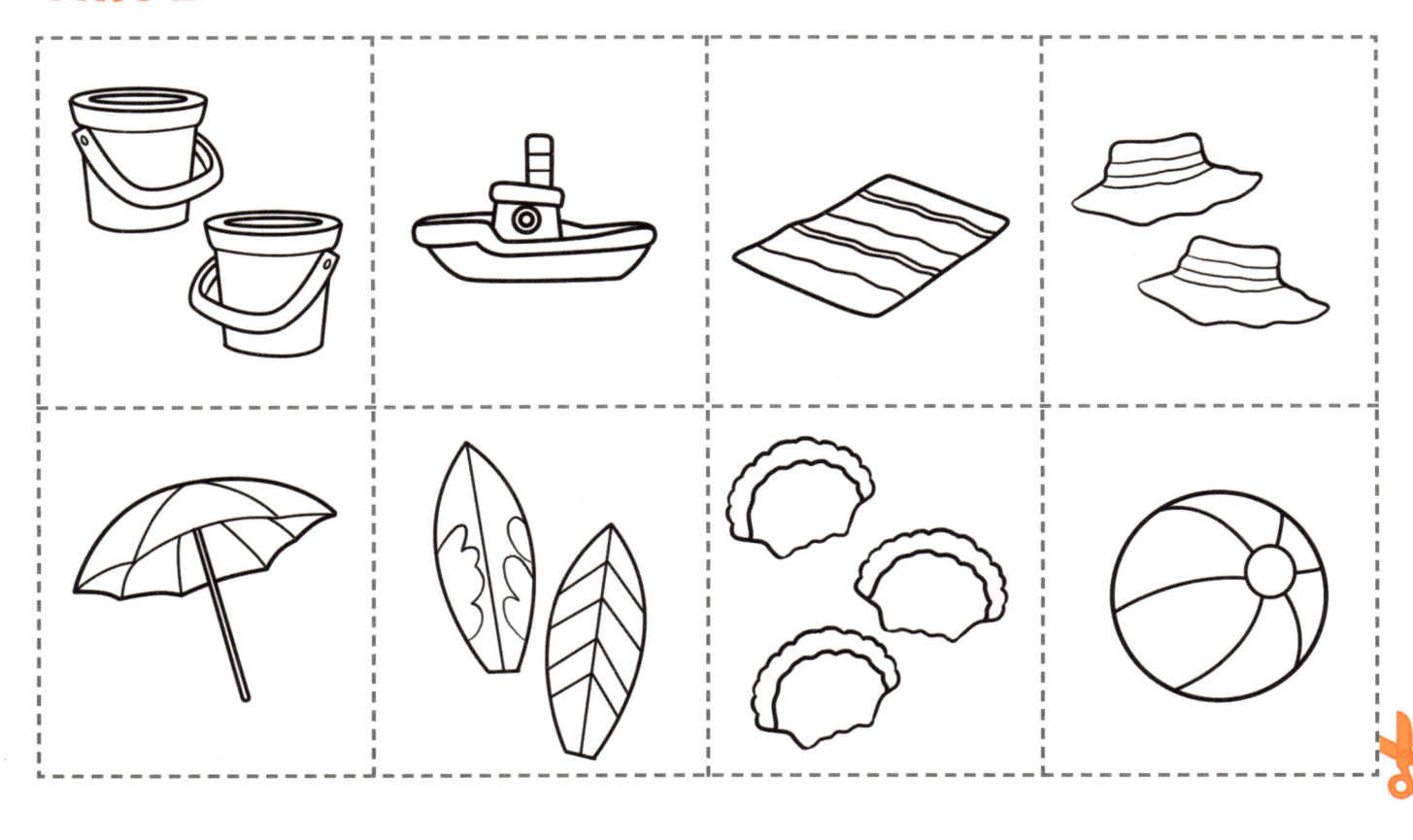

Unit 1

| Adam | Dexter | Dakota | Lucia |
| Hassan | Frank | Bella | Annie |

Unit 2

Unit 3

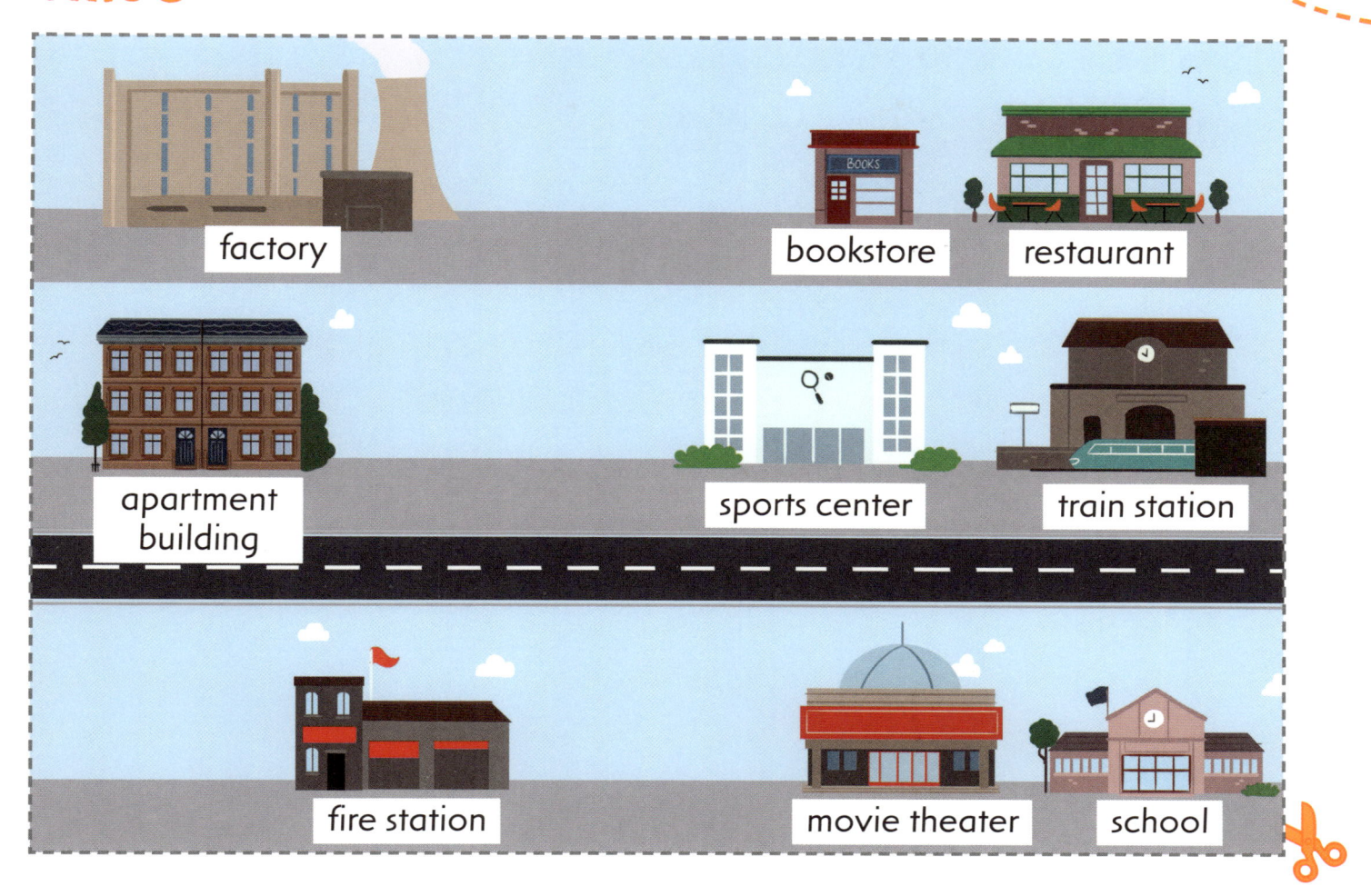

Cut outs

factory	bookstore	restaurant
apartment building	sports center	train station
fire station	movie theater	school

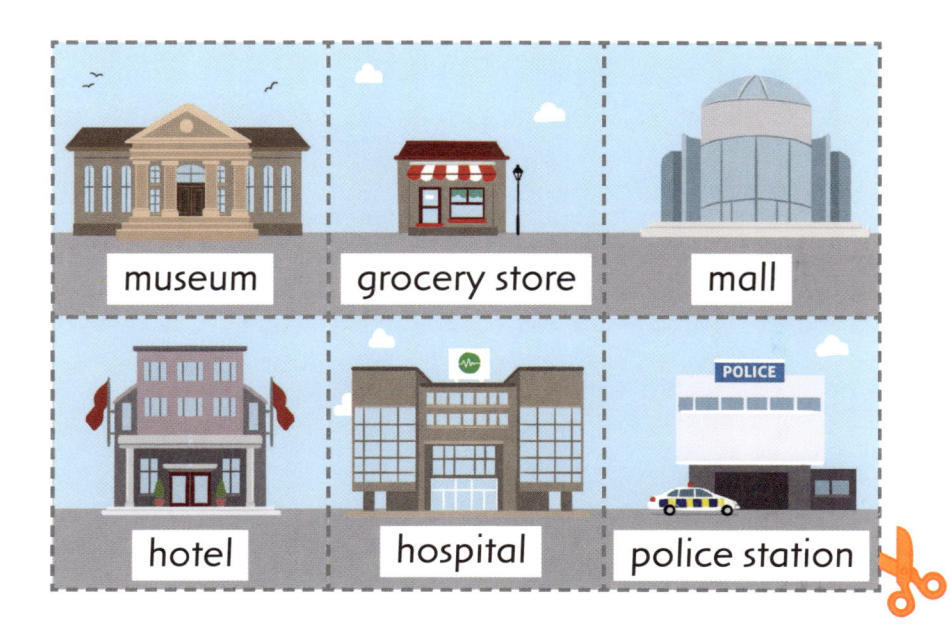

museum	grocery store	mall
hotel	hospital	police station

Unit 4

Cut outs

Unit 5

Cut outs

spring

summer

winter

fall

Unit 6

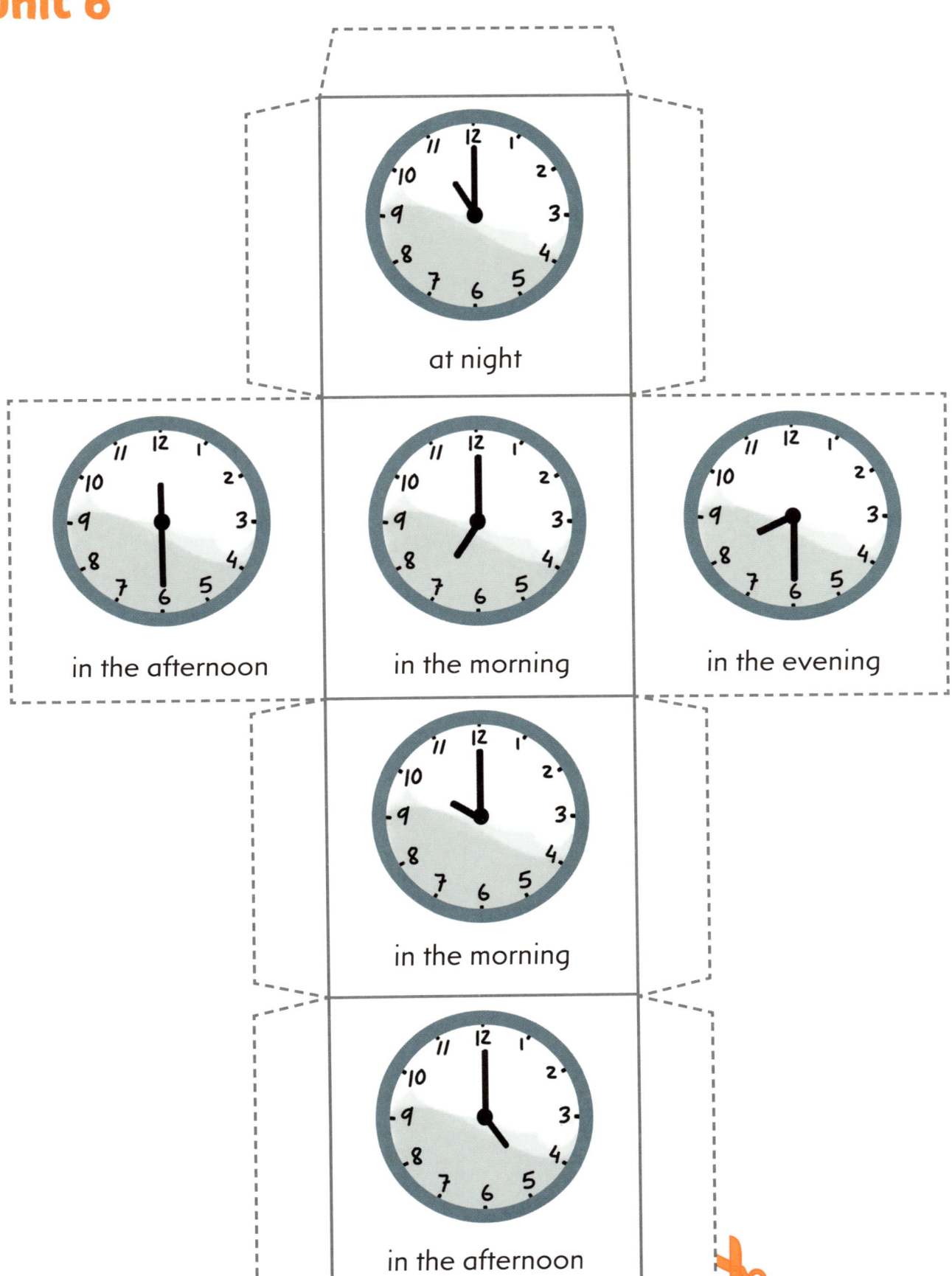

Cut outs

at night

in the afternoon

in the morning

in the evening

in the morning

in the afternoon

Unit 7

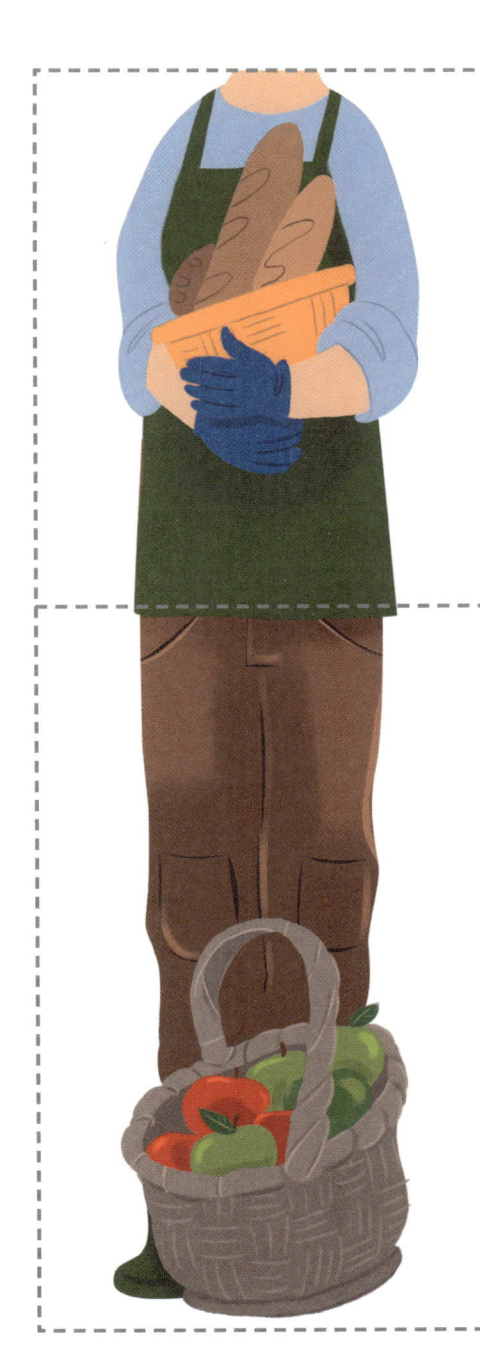

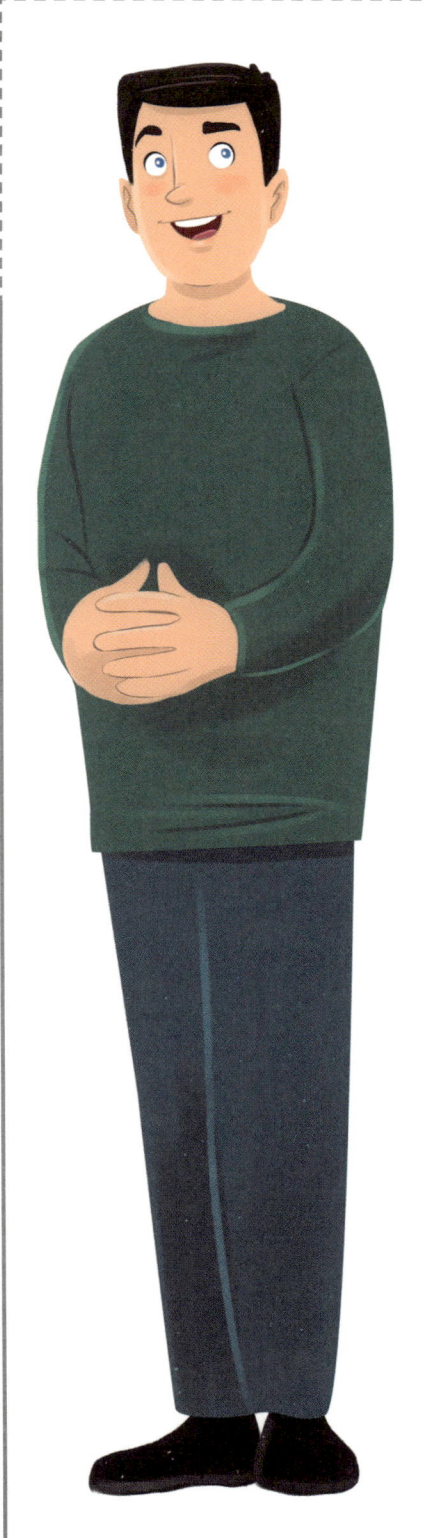

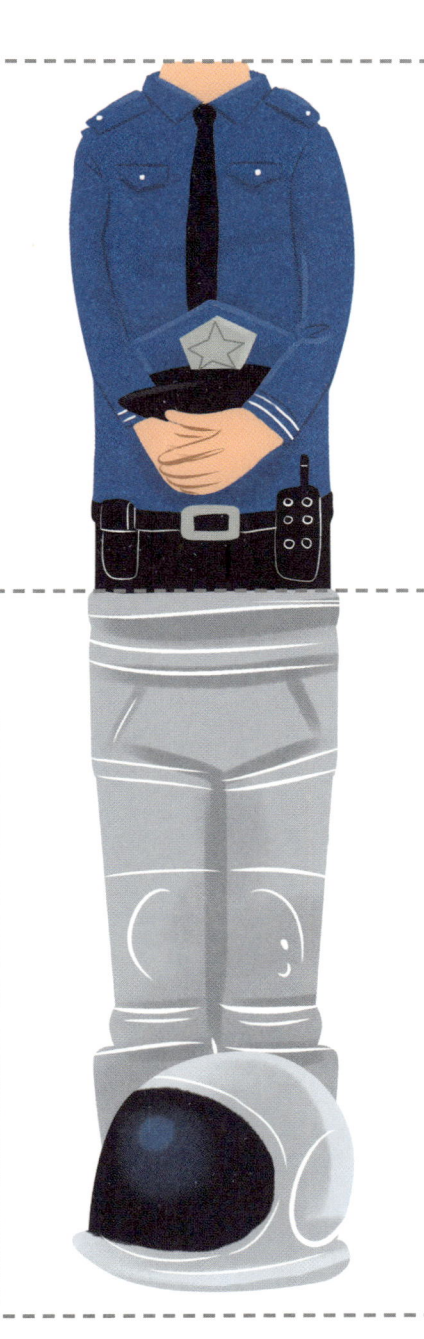

Cut outs

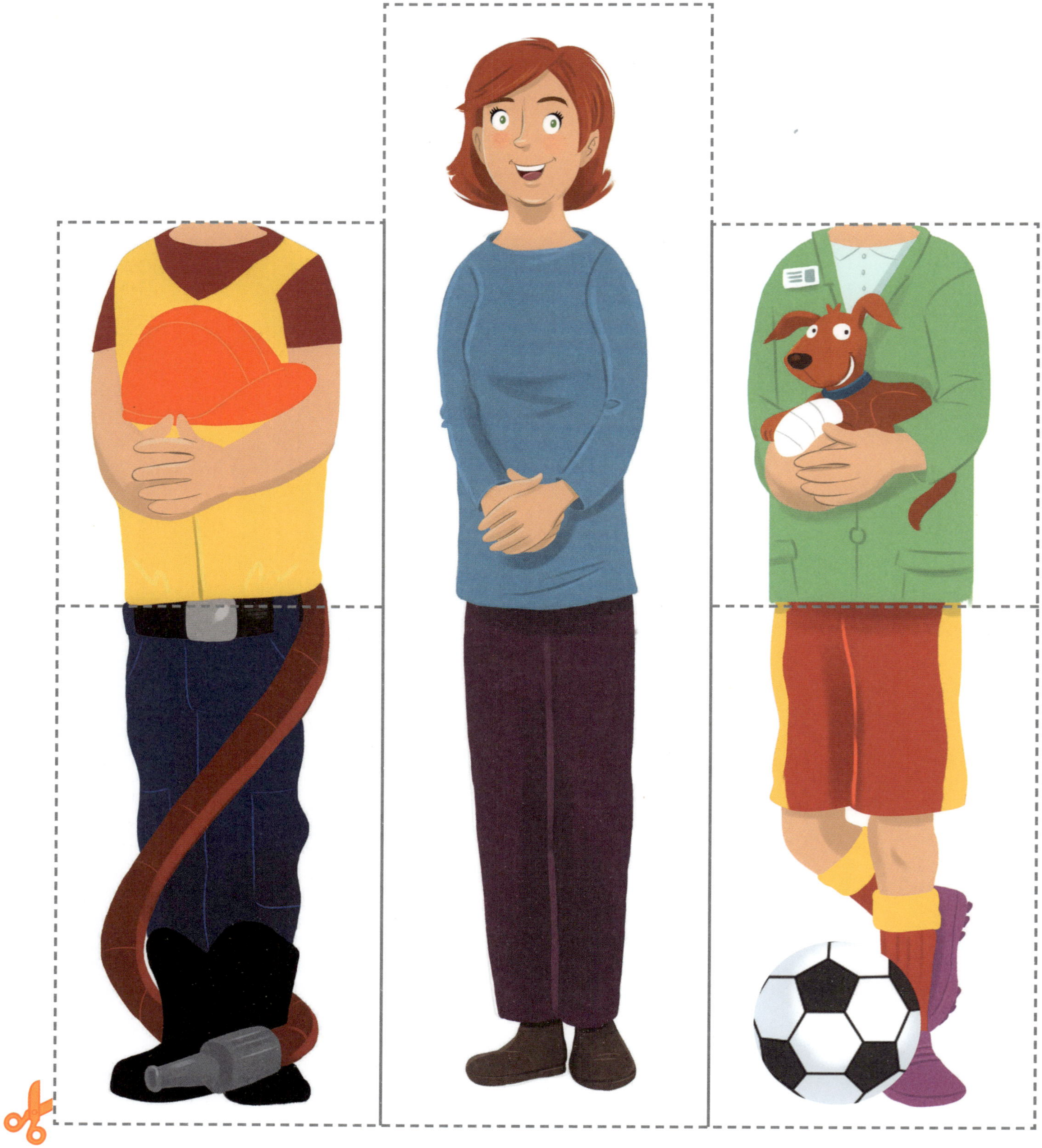

Unit 8

Cut outs

| Ben | Sam | Lin | Mei | Eva | Amy |

Unit 9

Cut outs

Jenny · Nathan · Jun · Avi · Leila · Nadia